Elizabeth W. Champney

Three Vassar Girls in Russia and Turkey

Elizabeth W. Champney

Three Vassar Girls in Russia and Turkey

ISBN/EAN: 9783743317024

Manufactured in Europe, USA, Canada, Australia, Japa

Cover: Foto ©ninafisch / pixelio.de

Manufactured and distributed by brebook publishing software (www.brebook.com)

Elizabeth W. Champney

Three Vassar Girls in Russia and Turkey

Three Vassar Girls

IN

Russia and Turkey.

BY

ELIZABETH W. CHAMPNEY,

AUTHOR OF "A NEGLECTED CORNER OF EUROPE," "THREE VASSAR GIRLS ABROAD," "THREE VASSAR GIRLS IN ENGLAND," ETC.

ILLUSTRATED BY "CHAMP"
AND OTHER DISTINGUISHED ARTISTS.

BOSTON:
ESTES AND LAURIAT,
PUBLISHERS.

CONTENTS.

CHAPTER		PAGE
I.	Lord Saunters .	11
II.	Sallie .	21
III.	Lady Saunters .	29
IV.	An Unexpected Meeting . . .	38
V.	A Newspaper Correspondent and a Trip to Ragusa .	42
VI.	The Adventures Begin . .	58
VII.	Montenegro	71
VIII.	Lord Saunters is taken Prisoner	93
IX.	Melicent and Captain Müller . .	104
X.	Greece	113
XI.	First Impressions of Turkey . . .	131
XII.	St. Petersburg	151
XIII.	Balkan Roses	168
XIV.	Moscow, Nijni-Novgorod, and the Crimea .	186
XV.	Shipka Pass	211
XVI.	Plevna, and the Passage of the Balkans .	230

ILLUSTRATIONS.

	PAGE
With the Red Cross	*Frontispiece*
Lord Saunters and Gus	12
Gibraltar	13
Lord Beaconsfield	15
Spanish Donna	17
Russian Arms	20
Sallie	21
Gus	21
Greece	24
The Propylea	25
Lady Saunters	29
Algernon Saunters	31
The Hippodrome	35
An Unexpected Meeting	38
Captain Müller	39
Piazza del Duomo—Court of Diocletian's Palace	45
Ragusa	49
Mr. Norcross	51
Peasant Girls	53
Correspondents on their way to Peco Pavlovitch's Camp	59
The War Correspondent	61
Council of War at Peco Pavlovitch's Camp	63
A Barbarous Operation	66
Insurgents in Ambush	67
Departed Glories	69
Cousin Trajan	72
Montenegrin Senator	73
Montenegrin Scenes	77
Montenegrin Soldier	81
Prince Nicholas	84
Princess Milene	85
Mr. Ignatieff	86
Montenegrins	87
A Turkish Commander	94
Bashi-Bazouks	95
Portico of a Cottage in Montenegro	99
Mr. Norcross looked up	101

	PAGE
Church of Perchtoldsdorf	105
A Russian Police Agent	107
Castle of Eisgrub	108
Melicent	109
The Danube at Linz	110
Ionic and Corinthian Columns	116
Sports of Ancient Greece	117
Penelope	118
In Doubt	119
Modern Athens from the Acropolis	121
Caryatides	123
The Parthenon	125
The Temple of the Wingless Victory	127
At the Museum	129
Sketches at Constantinople	133
Lord Saunters depressed	135
Gus's Idea of Mr. Humphrey	135
Mr. Humphrey appears	136
English insulted in Constantinople	137
Student of Robert College	141
Monument in the British Graveyard, Scutari	143
A Family Corner—Turkish Cemetery, Scutari	144
Abd-ul-Aziz	145
Mourad V.	145
Tomb of Sultan Mahmoud's Favorite Horse	146
Bashi-Bazouks	147
Drosky-driver	151
St. Isaac's Church	152
Bird's-eye View of St. Petersburg	153
Statue of Peter the Great	155
Nicholas Bridge	157
The Countess Melinoff	159
Mrs. Davenport	159
The Winter Palace	160
The Grand Duke Nicholas	161
Dimitri Dimitrievitch	162

ILLUSTRATIONS.

	PAGE
A Military Review	163
A Suspicious Interview	166
A Marriage Procession in Bulgaria	171
The Rose Harvest	173
Interior of Bulgarian Peasant Dwelling	175
Princess Nathalie	177
Prince Milan IV. of Servia	178
Servians	179
Two Ways of Wearing Veils	183
Bucharest	184
Alexander II., Czar of Russia	187
A Well-Known Figure	190
The Granovitaya Palace	193
Melicent is surprised	194
Czar Kolokol	195
Church of Vasili Blagennoy	197
Calmuck Tartar Maid	205
The Old Diplomat	209
The Epaulets returned	211
Russian Military Types	214
Cossacks on the Road from Galatz	215
Russian Officers taking the Turkish Flag	219
The Red Cross at Work	223
Reception of the Czar by the Clergy	225
Passage of Balkans	231
Forgotten	234
Turkish Crone	235
Relieving the Guard at Shipka	237

THREE VASSAR GIRLS IN RUSSIA AND TURKEY.

THREE VASSAR GIRLS

IN

RUSSIA AND TURKEY.

CHAPTER I.

LORD SAUNTERS.

IT was at Gibraltar, in the autumn of 1875, that Sallie and Gus first met Lord Saunters and his family.

The steamer stopped here to coal after its long trip across the Atlantic; and the passengers had an opportunity to land and to inspect the fortifications constructed by the English, the famous galleries in the Rock, with their great guns commanding the strait and the Spanish shore.

The varied nationalities to be found in the streets and markets were extremely interesting. Here a Moor from Africa, in a white burnous, stalked majestically by, hardly brushing with his robe the cringing Jew who flattened himself against the wall to let him pass. In this corner sat a jetty Nubian displaying for sale a basket of pomegranates; and there two Spanish ladies, with lace mantillas thrown over their shapely heads, waved their fans gently at a jaunty English officer in a gay scarlet and gold uniform; and marching down another steep street to the sound of a wheezy bagpipe was a company of Scotch Highlanders; while the flags of a dozen nations waved from the shipping in the harbor, all dominated by the power of England.

"England was pretty 'cute to secure this toll-gate to the Mediterranean — now, wasn't she?" Gus remarked, as they steamed away.

"England is usually pretty 'cute in her dealings with the foreign powers," said a pompous-looking gentleman in a long gray duster, who happened to be standing just behind Gus.

He was a new passenger, who had just come on board with his family and quite a suite of attendants. Gus looked up quickly, a little taken aback, for he saw instantly that the speaker was an Englishman, though he wore a beard instead of the characteristic mutton-chop whiskers. The light veil twisted around his hat and the " Murray's

LORD SAUNTERS AND GUS.

Guide Book" protruding from one of the side pockets of the Russia leather travelling-bag proclaimed his nationality, while the crest engraved on the gold handle of his umbrella and the obsequious deference shown him implied that he was a "milord."

Gus straightened himself, and strove to be equal to the occasion. "I have always admired the policy of England as exhibited by her colonial possessions," he replied, with a dignity which quite matched that of the Briton. "I think that you English have treated the North American Indian much more fairly than we have."

GIBRALTAR.

The strange gentleman smiled. "You are doubtless an American," he said, "though I hardly expected to find an admission from one of your nation that England excelled America in anything. I fear, too,

LORD BEACONSFIELD.

that whatever humanity we may have exercised to the natives of our colonies is more a matter of policy on our part than of principle."

"Is not humanity always the best policy, sir?"

"Well, no: a long experience in the diplomatic service has hardly taught me that. I have made the Eastern Question the study of my life, and the policy of England seems to be inextricably intertwined with the permanence of the Turkish power; and the Turks, you know, are not noted for their humanity."

"Now, that is just what I want to know more about!" Gus exclaimed eagerly. "The Eastern Question — what is it? We see so much about it in the papers nowadays. Is there going to be a war in Turkey? Excuse me, sir, but I am very deeply interested. You see, my sister and I are going to Turkey, and of course I would like to know whether it will be quite safe for her to stay; and if you are in the diplomatic service you must know what England is going to do."

The gentleman smiled at the boy's eagerness and volubility. "I am not at liberty to divulge any state secrets," he said, "but of this at least I can assure you, there will be no war in Turkey this year. My friend, Lord Beaconsfield, heads the pro-Turkish party in the English cabinet, and will control the policy of England. All sympathy with this petty insurrection in Herzegovina is mere stuff and nonsense. It is possibly true that the Turks are a little hard on the European provinces, but any talk of atrocities is mere Russian humbug. The situation is just this: Russia and England are each extending their possessions into Asia, and are formidable rivals. Turkey stands in Russia's way; and it is England's policy to help Turkey. Russia would like to incite the Turkish possessions in Europe to rebellion, and assist in breaking up the Turkish Empire; but, my boy, England will not permit it." The gentleman brought his jaws together with a snap. He had evidently perfect faith in England's power to rule the universe. The boy's face fell. "Then, it will be perfectly safe for us to travel in European Turkey?" he asked, with a not very happy expression of countenance, — "no chance of the Servians rising, or any Turkish massacres, or that sort of thing?"

"Not the least. Mukhtar Pacha will soon put an end to the present trouble in Herzegovina, and peace will be restored."

Gus sighed. "Sallie will be glad," he said slowly: "she's dead set against war."

SPANISH DONNA.

"Who is Sallie?"

"She is my sister, sir."

"A missionary?"

"Oh, dear, no! We are travelling for pleasure, sir, and information. — not that Sallie needs it in the least. She was at Paris with friends at the time of the siege. I have always been provoked to think that I was not old enough to be with her. She is on her way now to join these same friends, — Mrs. Davenport and her daughter Melicent, who have been living abroad all this time, and are at Vienna. I don't think I shall care anything about them, for they are very stylish people, and society people are always sure to be stupid, you know; but there is another friend of Sallie's down in European Turkey, who is a missionary, and we want to get to her, if we can, and persuade her to come back. It was awfully foolish of her to go out there, Sallie thinks, and dangerous too; and that's why I've been boring you with all these questions."

"You have not annoyed me at all, my boy," replied the Englishman. "You seem to be a very plucky pair of young people. I would like to meet your sister, and you will, perhaps, do me the honor of presenting me to her."

Gus hesitated. He had run on with perfect freedom; but introducing this stranger to his sister was another matter. "I — I — Sallie is rather shy about meeting strangers; that is, she is very busy mornings, and she always takes a nap in the afternoon," he stammered.

"I see," the elder gentleman replied good-naturedly. "You are quite right: it is not good form to be too intimate with unknown people. Possibly my wife may be more successful with your sister than I. I like you all the better for your care of her. There is the dinner-bell. Join me on deck whenever you care to do so. My son Algernon is quite an Orientalist, and he will enjoy talking with you about Turkey."

Lord Saunters seemed to have a mania of dislike for the Russian coat-of-arms. They saw the flag flying on a Russian vessel as they steamed away from Gibraltar, and he remarked that the two-headed monstrosity seemed more like a great, greedy vulture to him than an eagle. He told with evident relish the story of the Russian prince who, in hunting, brought down a bird, and inquired of his attendants what manner of wild-fowl this was.

"Your Highness has killed an eagle," replied the squire.

"Oh, no!" exclaimed the prince, whose knowledge of ornithology was largely derived from the royal arms, "you cannot deceive me. Do I not see that it has only one head!"

Having finished his story with a cordial nod, the old man ambled briskly away.

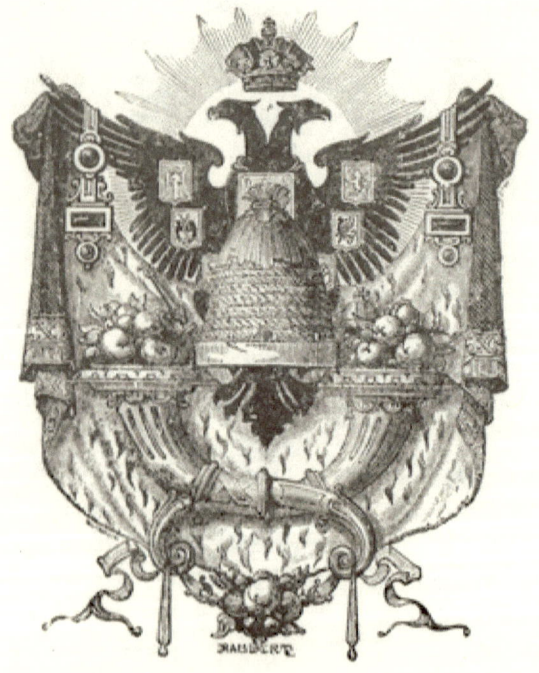

RUSSIAN ARMS.

CHAPTER II.

SALLIE.

SALLIE.

THE tour which Sallie and her brother were now taking had only been decided upon after long deliberation. Gus had finished his preparation for college and had successfully passed the Harvard examinations; but his father thought him too young to enter, and it was decided that European travel would advantageously fill in the interim.

Neither Mr. nor Mrs. Benton could conveniently leave home; but as Sallie had travelled in Europe before this, and was a girl of clear judgment as well as something of a stickler for the proprieties, they had perfect confidence in their daughter's ability to conduct such a tour, and everything had been left to her management. Gus had, at first, manifested little enthusiasm.

"You had such a nice time in Paris," he said, "that you will want to go there again, and I hate French and despise shopping."

"Gus dear, you are quite wrong," his sister had replied. "I haven't a bit of shopping to do, and just because I have been to Paris I do not care to go again. 'Fresh fields and pastures new,' say I."

GUS.

"And I know what that means," Gus replied moodily: "you mean to go to Germany, and if there is anything I dislike more than French it's German. There never was a better thing written than what Mark

Twain said about German grammar, with its compound nouns and its genders and cases and all that nonsense. Sounds like a parcel of horses talking; but those German officers were so polite when you got caught within their lines during the siege of Paris that I've no doubt you're pining to hie away to the banks of the Rhine and see your Von Lindenthals and your Lieutenant Schwarzes and your precious Captain Müllers once more."

Sallie flushed indignantly. "Germany is just the one country I insist on not visiting," she replied dryly, "and Captain Müller the very last man whom I desire to meet."

Gus looked at her in surprise. "You don't say!" he remarked, and then there was silence between them for the space of just one minute, during which brief time Sallie mentally reviewed her last European tour, and especially her stay in Versailles with Madame de Beaumont while the great German army was waiting for the surrender of Paris. She thought of the kindness of the German officers who were quartered at Madame de Beaumont's, of the respect and consideration shown to them both during those terrible days of siege, — of Captain Müller's honest face, and of something he had said to her, and then she flushed indignantly as she thought, "No, no, he never really loved me, or he would have been willing to leave the army for my sake when I told him that I thought it was wicked, and could never marry a soldier."

"Oh! were you speaking? what did you say, Gus?" she asked, as she awoke from her reverie.

"I asked you to deign to indicate a country which you would like to visit."

"It really doesn't matter, dear. We are sure to have a good time, you and I together, anywhere. Where would you like to go?"

"If I had my own way I would take a cruise with Captain Kidd to the Cannibal Islands. Since that is not possible, if there is to be war anywhere in Europe let us choose that country."

Sallie was silent for a moment, and then replied, —

"The papers say that the situation is a little cloudy in Turkey."

She mentioned the country not quite at random. Alice was in Turkey, and she felt sure that this was a country where she would be quite sure not to meet Captain Müller, little dreaming that her fate (or was it not Providence?) was leading directly toward the meeting which she wished to avoid.

"Well, let's choose Turkey, then," Gus replied. "I want to go somewhere where there is a chance for adventure, and I don't want to do the every-day, regulation thing when I go to Europe. What the papers say sounds promising; maybe we can get kidnapped by some of the bandits, or we may tumble into a battle somewhere."

"War is a frightful thing," said Sallie musingly. "I saw more than I wanted of it at Versailles. I hope that there never will be another war on the face of the earth, but there is one reason why I would like to go to European Turkey."

"I know. You would like to do Greece on the way. It would be nice for your art to stop at Athens and sketch the Acropolis. Well, I'll stand it, if you will promise on your sacred honor not to make the visit an instructive one."

"I would like to stop in Greece very much," Sallie admitted, "but my dearest friend, Alice Newton, has gone out to Turkey somewhere as a missionary."

Gus whistled. "It must be an uncommonly stupid sort of a life," he said.

"Yes," Sallie replied, "I am afraid it is. Dear Alice was a saint; one of the loveliest girls I ever knew. If she had been a Romanist, she would have taken the veil. As she was a Presbyterian, she did the nearest thing to it which she could, and renounced the world with all its pomps and vanities. I was very angry with her for becoming a missionary; but her mother died, and her father married again, and she hadn't any younger sisters to fit for Vassar, or a brother to plague her and to plague in turn, and, I have no doubt, she felt as if there was no room for her in the world."

"Done!" exclaimed Gus. "We will go to Turkey, and, if you want to, on the way we will take in Greece. I'll loaf around Mars Hill

GREECE.

while you are making your sketches, and see if I can scare up a few adventures with the bandits, and then we will go to Turkey and hunt up your missionary friend and rescue her. I've no doubt that she is sick of the country by this time, and we will bring her back in triumph, and you and she shall set up a studio together in Boston. You said she used to paint when you were in France together, didn't you? I

THE PROPYLEA.

shall run in to see you every Saturday, and get you to translate my Greek for me, and we will have no end of fun."

"That is a fine prospect," laughed Sallie, "only I am afraid we shall not be able to persuade Alice into it. If she has given up art, it is because she considers it her duty to be a missionary, and Alice always placed duty before everything else. However, we will try our best, for I like your plan, Gus, very much indeed. It would be delightful only to see her again, and talk of the days when we were Three Vassar Girls in France."

"Where is your third crony, Miss Davenport?"

"Melicent and her mother are in Vienna. I would like very much to visit them on our way to Bulgaria.

"Perhaps Mrs. Davenport and Melicent would go with us; that would simplify everything."

"Humph! I don't know about that. We don't want too many women; besides, I thought that Miss Davenport was married to the war correspondent, Mr. Osborne."

"War correspondents do not make money enough to marry upon so quickly; and, though Melicent is wealthy, James Osborne is too much of a man to allow her to support him. When I last heard from her, he had gone with the Russians, on the Khivan campaign, into the heart of Asia."

"He must be a plucky sort of fellow. If there should be a war in Turkey, don't you think that he would probably be sent there?"

"He would, doubtless, be there; but I fancy we would not, for father and mother would insist on our leaving the country in case hostilities were declared."

"Pshaw! I hadn't thought of that; but perhaps we will be lucky enough to get caught, as you were in the German lines."

The plans thus discussed crystallized in due time. Friends had been found who were going to Vienna, and for the sake of the supposed advantage of their company Sallie had determined to make the visit to Melicent first.

A sea voyage is a great revealer of latent selfishness; and the Greysons, their fellow-travellers, proved to be a greater trial than comfort.

It was on the autumn day that we have described, that Gus enjoyed his first glimpse of Europe, at Gibraltar. He had told Sallie of his interview with Lord Saunters, but had wisely omitted to report his lordship's request for an introduction, fearing that his sister would think him indiscreet. He secretly felt that he had been too familiar, and resolved to avoid this fault in future.

CHAPTER III.

LADY SAUNTERS.

LADY SAUNTERS.

SALLIE encountered the English lady on the following day. Lady Saunters had evidently had a line of conduct suggested to her by her husband, for she was seen by Gus to make vigorous signs of interrogation across the table to her liege on the American girl's appearance at breakfast. Sallie went immediately on deck after the meal, and my lady soon after followed. She looked at the young people irresolutely, and sank into her steamer-chair.

"She makes me think of Sennacherib," Gus remarked, "with his costume all glittering with purple and gold."

"Byron says 'cohorts,' not 'costume,'" corrected Sallie.

"Never mind Sennacherib. There she is, and if she isn't bearing down on us this minute, like the wolf on the fold!"

The lady had, in fact, risen, and, accelerated by the pitching of the ship, was sidling rapidly toward them. She caught at the rail, righted herself, and affably extended a small, enamelled bonbonnière, which Sallie at first mistook for a snuff-box.

"Peptic lozenges, my dear," she explained, — "a specific against sea-sickness."

Sallie good-humoredly partook of a lozenge. There was something in the lady's voice which was strangely familiar, and she looked at her inquiringly.

"My husband tells me that you are an American, my dear; and as we travelled in America two years ago, and met with such uniform courtesy everywhere, especially from a family by the name of Benton, whom we met in the Yellowstone Park, who rescued us from great annoyance "—

Sallie gave a gasp of surprise. "Lady Saunters!" she exclaimed, "do you not recognize me?"

Her ladyship raised her lorgnette. "It is, no, surely it cannot be, little Sallie Benton?"

"Have I grown old so rapidly, dear Lady Saunters? But, indeed, I can hardly tell you how pleasant it seems to meet a friend."

"It is very agreeable for us as well, my dear. We have just come from England, and are on our way to Athens, where we expect to remain until the arrival of the Prince of Wales on his way to India. The Prince has invited my second son, Algernon, to go out with him. Alfred, our eldest, is in England. We have plenty of time, and intend first to make a little stop at Venice and at Trieste."

"My brother and I are also on our way to Trieste," Sallie remarked, "so our journey lies for a little way in the same direction. We may possibly visit Greece later. Perhaps you can kindly give me some information in regard to Athens."

The American college for the study of the Greek language and archæology, of whose advantages Vassar girls have now a right to avail themselves, was not then established at Athens, and Sallie felt quite doubtful as to this part of her trip.

"If you were only ready to go on to Greece now, my dear," Lady Saunters replied, "I might be able to be of some service to you; and it seems to me a serious undertaking for a young woman to travel about alone. However, now that we have fallen in together, and our routes lie in the same direction, I shall be pleased to afford you any protection in my power."

Sallie colored: she was inclined to feel indignant, but she recognized the fact that her ladyship's remarks were meant kindly, and had a show of reason. She explained that they were nominally under the care of the Greysons, but that, so far, they had proved a great care to her, and she would be very happy when she could exchange Mrs. Greyson's chaperonage for that of Mrs. Davenport.

"Exchange it now for mine, my dear!" exclaimed Lady Saunters. "I will explain to Mrs. Greyson that I am the friend of your mamma, and I am sure that she will be satisfied with our credentials."

As Sallie knew that her parents had been pleasantly impressed by Lord and Lady Saunters, the arrangement was quickly made. Lady Saunters was peculiar, but she was good, and Sallie was grateful for the opportunity of availing herself of the companionship of a lady older and more experienced than herself. Lord Saunters was duly presented, and Algernon, who was an extremely well-bred young man, with a listless, world-weary air, to which Sallie at once took mental exception. "I do not like you," she said to herself: "you are a prig, and we shall not get on at all."

ALGERNON SAUNTERS.

While she was registering this prophecy, Algernon Saunters was thinking, "What a bore that mother should have taken it into her head to pick up this young person, with her disagreeably American manner! I shall have as little to do with her as possible."

He accordingly retired to the cabin, where he devoted himself to writing up his journal,—an occupation in which he always intrenched himself when menaced with uncongenial company. The others grew to understand this, and Gus would say, "He is seeking the seclusion which his journal grants."

Gus had not taken the Yellowstone trip, and he was much surprised when Lord Saunters claimed Sallie as an old acquaintance. "Never mind, my boy," said his lordship: "you were right, quite right, in guarding your sister."

They were transferred at Palermo to another steamer, bound up the Adriatic to Venice. Sallie was pleased to find that Lord and Lady Saunters planned to spend two days here; and visions of floating about the city in a gondola, of visiting St. Mark's and the Ducal Palace, danced through her brain. But this was not Lady Saunters's errand in Venice. She had stopped simply to buy some Venetian point-lace. Algernon Saunters also expressed his antipathy for Venice. "Such a beastly, damp place, you know. I can never get over the feeling that the city is suffering from an inundation."

When Gus inquired if he meant to visit the picture galleries, he replied that no one ever went that dreary round but once, to be able to say that he had seen this and that, and that he was thankful that a conscientious governess had dragged him through the pilgrimage at the mature age of six, and that one of the penances of life was performed.

In spite of thereby confessing that she was visiting Venice for the first time, Sallie bravely visited the principal places of interest, remaining so long entranced before Titian's masterpieces that she was late to dinner; but, altogether, the glimpse at Venice was a very unsatisfactory one.

"I wish we could stay a month here," said Gus.

"Yes," replied Sallie regretfully, "and I presume that at the end of the month we would want still more to remain a year. And what would become of our Turkish expedition?"

As they embarked for Trieste, Algernon Saunters admitted that he would have preferred making a trip across the Adriatic to the little republic of Montenegro. "Why, that is supposed to be a hot-bed of revolt and conspiracy against the Turks," said Gus.

"True," replied the young man; "and for that very reason I have a great curiosity to see these plucky Montenegrins, who, in their little, star-shaped republic, a mere pinhead on the map of Europe, have defied the Turkish power so long and so successfully."

Sallie looked up with surprise; it was the first time that Algernon had expressed interest in any subject.

"They have set a most mischievous example to Herzegovina and Servia," Lord Saunters remarked, "and are really the spark in the great gunpowder mine which would shake all Europe but for the repressing hand of Great Britain."

"That is it," remarked Algernon. "I have a haunting feeling that if I should look into this matter I would inevitably find myself interested in the under dog in the fight; and might even come out on the wrong side of British interests, which would never do, you know. My only safety as a member of a conservative family lies in ignorance."

"It seems to me," said Sallie hesitatingly, "that a high position and wide influence such as yours involve you in grave responsibility. I do not see how you dare to neglect investigating such a matter."

Algernon flushed slightly. "It is fortunate for my peace of mind that I do not possess your morbidly active American conscience," he remarked coldly.

Sallie bit her lip. She felt that she had said too much; but Gus could not take the hint, and continued impulsively, "I think, Lord Saunters, that there is something magnificent in those Montenegrins maintaining their independence in that way, and I don't see why England objects to the Servians and Bulgarians forming independent states, if they want to so much."

"Ah! that is the Eastern Question again," replied Lord Saunters.

"You Americans are mad on the subject of independence, but there are other considerations involved here, of far greater importance. As Mr. Pitt so well explained, England's policy it is to preserve the balance of power in Europe. No matter what may be the atrocities of the Turks, their power must be bolstered up by England, or there will be no barrier in the way of Russia's advance into Asia, and her ultimate seizure of our empire in India."

Gus whistled. "So that's the idea," he said; "but wouldn't India be just as well off under Russian as under English rule?"

Lord Saunters turned purple; and Lady Saunters, who had been rummaging in her reticule, handed her husband some pellets.

"Now, my dear," she remarked persuasively, "you know you always take *Nux* when Mr. Gladstone speaks. Really, Master Benton, I must request you not to bring up these exciting topics. It is almost as bad for my husband as attendance on Parliament. His physician has absolutely prohibited politics on this trip,—politics and pork-pie, and my poor husband is so devoted to both."

Lady Saunters's care of her husband would have been touching if it had been less absurd. For some reason not understood by the Bentons, she imagined that Friday was a more trying day for her husband than any other. It may have been the day on which, when in England, he devoted most attention to parliamentary debates. Gus pretended to imagine that Lady Saunters belonged to a new order of religionists, similar to the Seventh-day Baptists, and that she observed Friday as a sacred day of rest. Certainly she kept it with a more than Sabbatical rigidity.

On Friday, at breakfast, Lady Saunters watched her husband's plate with a keenness which must have been very exasperating to her victim.

"No fish," she would say to the waiter. "It is a relic of Romish superstition to eat fish on Friday. Besides, fish contains phosphorus, and is very stimulating to the brain."

THE HIPPODROME.

"My dear" (this to her husband), "you are surely not going to take curry; you know it is Friday."

On Friday, Lady Saunters substituted readings from translations of Latin authors or from Hamerton's "Intellectual Life," which she carried with her, for the morning newspaper.

"The newspapers," she confided to Sallie, "so often irritate my husband, while I have observed that readings from Virgil, *my* readings especially, are apt to have a soothing and sleep-inducing effect."

Lady Saunters's readings frequently produced a desire to sleep in all who heard her. Her husband invariably covered his patient visage with his handkerchief at the beginning of this ordeal, and sleep soon rescued him from the infliction. These Friday readings were uninterrupted by sea or land travel, and it was entirely owing to the fact that the day after their arrival in Trieste happened to be a Friday that Sallie met Captain Müller.

"What pleased you most in Venice?" Algernon Saunters asked of Gus.

"The bronze horses of Lysippus," the boy replied, "above the Cathedral of St. Mark's."

"If you go to Constantinople," said the young man, "you will see the hippodrome where they once stood beside the race-track of the Emperor Constantine surrounded by the best chariot horses of the empire, where the donkeys of the Mussulman now congregate."

CHAPTER IV.

AN UNEXPECTED MEETING.

SALLIE had mentioned to Lady Saunters at breakfast that she was hungry for some American newspapers.

"Sh!" exclaimed my lady, pointing to her husband; and after breakfast Lady Saunters explained that on any other day she would have asked her husband to send for them to the office of the Austrian Lloyd's Steamship Company.

AN UNEXPECTED MEETING.

"Gus and I can get them," said Sallie; "we would like the walk."

"I fancy nothing can happen to you," she said dubiously, as they set out.

Gus laughed heartily as soon as they were out of hearing. "The very idea of anything happening to you, Sallie!"

"It is absurd," she replied, "but the good woman means it kindly."

They walked down the Corso, the principal thoroughfare, and found their way after a time to the Tergesteum, so named from the ancient Roman name of the city, a handsome building containing the steamer offices, a grand ball-room, and several reading-rooms.

"I wonder whether ladies are admitted," queried Sallie.

"I will find out," said Gus, and he accosted an officer who was passing. This gentleman turned politely, and was about to give the desired information when his eye fell upon Sallie, and he stopped in the middle of his sentence, a look of the utmost surprise on his features. Sallie in turn gave a little gasp, and then laughed merrily.

"Why, Captain Müller!" she exclaimed, "you are the last man that I expected to meet here." "Or wanted to," added Gus, under his breath. But, for a young woman who had certainly made this announcement, Miss Sallie's behavior during the next hour or so was most contradictory and mystifying.

Captain Müller, recovering from his astonishment, offered to show them the Tergesteum; and, although Sallie professed herself deeply interested in everything, Gus ascertained afterward that she had paid no attention to the building. The inspection lasted a long time, and as they left, Sallie remarked that they were going to the Byzantine Cathedral in the old part of the city, and Captain Müller offered to show them the way. Gus was surprised that she should accept this offer, for they had looked out the way together on a map which Sallie had in her pocket at that moment. Moreover, it soon transpired that Captain Müller had never visited the cathedral, and that either he did not know the route or was purposely making it as long as possible; but when Gus suggested that his sister should refer to the map, the sly puss scowled at him in a manner which showed that she knew perfectly well what she was about. They reached the cathedral at last, but when

CAPTAIN MÜLLER.

Gus would have dragged them at once to the spot where the guide-book told them that the stones with old Roman inscriptions were built into the wall, Sallie declared that she was too tired to take another step, and seated herself in a corner sheltered by a confessional. There was no one in the church, and they chatted in a low tone, Gus remaining with them for a time, but finally strolled away to make a note of the inscriptions.

"And how does it happen that you are here in Trieste?" Sallie asked of the captain.

"I have a furlough," he explained, "and am visiting an aunt."

"Then you are still in the army?" He was not in uniform, and at first Sallie had presumed too much from this circumstance.

"Yes, I am still in the army. There is no other career open to me, you know. Do you still retain your prejudice against everything military?"

"Yes, I have grown to hate war more than ever, and I am sorry that a friend of mine should have adopted it as his profession."

Captain Müller was silent for a moment. He wanted to tell her that he had come to think as she did, and that he was ready, if she could only reward him by becoming his wife, to give up his commission and seek some other career, but it seemed to him that such a declaration would sound very abrupt, and that it ought to be worked up to. "My sister has married a Russian nobleman," he remarked, "and has offered to secure me a position in Russia. Do you think you will visit Russia? I would like to have you know my sister."

"You are very kind, but it is hardly possible. We are on our way now to visit Mrs. Davenport and her daughter, who are in Vienna."

"How I would like to see them again! You must let me bring my aunt to call upon you before you leave, and show you about Trieste."

"I am sorry, but we leave to-morrow."

"So soon? There is much that is interesting in this old Austrian seaport."

In spite of the fact that they were quite alone, their conversation was constrained. There was a great barrier between them, which each wished away, but neither knew how to remove. Gus came back with the inscriptions, and the opportunity was gone. "It is awfully late." he remarked. "What do you suppose Sennacherib will say?"

"Let me escort you to your hotel," said the captain.

"Indeed, there is no need of it," Sallie replied, hastily producing at this late juncture the map. "Gus and I are quite used to making our way about alone."

She spoke so earnestly that Captain Müller perceived that for some reason his company was not desired. They went down the steps of the cathedral together, and he bowed politely, saying simply, "*Auf wiedersehen.*"

His brain was in a tumult. He had thought that he had forgotten Sallie, but at this chance meeting all the old feelings rushed back tempestuously. "She must reverse her refusal," he said to himself. "I shall try again, and this time I shall succeed."

But what opportunity had he for a second trial? She had said that they were to leave Trieste on the next morning, presumably for Vienna. He consulted a railway guide, and quickly decided upon the train which they would probably take. He then purchased one first-class ticket for this train, and, returning to his aunt's residence, informed that astonished woman that he had just heard that his old general was in Vienna, and wished to see him there.

He quieted his uneasy conscience with the thought that he was willing to recognize Sallie as his commanding officer from this time forward, and he hoped with all his heart that she really wished to meet him.

Frau Müller bustled about packing her nephew's lunch-basket, with true Austrian providence. "Such a summons bodes good luck," she said pleasantly. "I should not be surprised if you were going to be promoted."

"I hope so," Captain Müller replied, a great light shining in his eyes.

CHAPTER V.

A NEWSPAPER CORRESPONDENT AND A TRIP TO RAGUSA.

SALLIE and Gus walked toward their hotel for some time in silence. Sallie was thinking self-reproachfully. "What a foolish girl I am! Captain Müller is still in the army, a fact that shows that he does not care for me. I did not intend ever to see him again. I must not, since meeting him can make me so unhappy."

Gus interrupted her reverie. "Sallie, I am ashamed of you!"

"Yes, Gus?"

"You have been behaving badly, and you know it. I did not think my sister was capable of flirting."

"Flirting!"

"I should like to know what else you call the way you have just been going on, — letting this German officer know where we are going, and when. I would not be surprised if we met him on the train to-morrow."

"Do you think so? I hope not. Really, Gus, I never wish to meet him again."

"So you have said before; but I must say that your actions hardly bear out your words, and I don't see how you are going to avoid it now."

"We might take a different train. We will change our plans in some way to avoid the meeting."

On arriving at the hotel, they found, much to their surprise, that Lord Saunters had arranged an excursion which exactly fitted into their present mood.

Lady Saunters looked flurried and anxious. "Such an unfortunate occurrence!" she confided to Sallie. "Algy has met an old friend, a newspaper correspondent, — think of it, my dear, of all persons in the world, — and has introduced him to his father, and he has been exciting him sadly. He actually proposes that we shall make a trip to Montenegro, to see those horrid conspirators."

"We can go very comfortably," Algernon insisted, "by a little steamer of the Austrian Lloyds which runs down the Dalmatian coast to Cattaro in four days. Then, I think that Miss Benton would enjoy the trip. She can return to Trieste with perfect safety, and it will give her something quite out of the common. Then, too, it is quite on our way to Athens. There is an excellent hotel at Cattaro, the Maria Teresa, and you ladies can remain there, if you prefer, while we make the horseback excursion to Montenegro, though I hope you will decide to accompany us. Mr. Osborne is a delightfully entertaining man. You ought to know him."

Sallie had never seen Algernon Saunters so enthusiastic, and he had certainly never before manifested the least interest in her plans; but she hardly noticed this circumstance, for her ear had caught a familiar name.

"Mr. Osborne!" she exclaimed. "Is it the war correspondent, James Osborne? He is an old acquaintance of mine also, and is to marry my friend, Melicent Davenport. He is one of the most disinterested and self-sacrificing of men. I am so glad that you are going with him! You will gain some entirely new ideas, I am sure, and you may be perfectly certain that whatever James Osborne tells you is reliable. He has such a sense of even-handed justice all round, and is never carried away by impulses."

Lord Saunters smiled, and my lady remarked incredulously, —

"But you are not at all certain that this newspaper correspondent whom my husband has picked up is the very perfect person of whom you are speaking. I have a horror of all newspaper men: they are perpetually turning one's preconceived notions upside down. I am positive that the world would be much better off without newspapers."

"My dear mother," remarked Algernon, "listen to what your favorite modern writer, Mr. Hamerton, says about them;" and Lord Saunters opened the "Intellectual Life" and read aloud, "'Newspapers are to the whole civilized world what the daily house-talk is to the members of a household; they keep up our daily interest in each other, they save us from the evils of isolation. To live as a member of the great white race, that has filled Europe and America and colonized or conquered whatever other territories it has been pleased to occupy, it is necessary that every man should read his daily newspaper. Why are the French peasants so bewildered and at sea, so out of place, in the modern world? It is because they never read a newspaper. And why are the inhabitants of the United States so much more capable of concerted political action, so much more alive and modern, so much more interested in new discoveries of all kinds, and capable of selecting and utilizing the best of them? It is because the newspaper penetrates everywhere.

"'In times when great historical events are passing before our eyes, the journalist is to the future historians what the African traveller is to the map-makers. His work is the fresh record of an eye-witness, and enables us to become ourselves spectators of the mighty drama of the world. Never was this service so well rendered as it is now, by correspondents who achieve heroic feats of bodily and mental prowess, exposing themselves to the greatest dangers, and writing much and well in circumstances the most unfavorable to literary composition. How vividly the English war correspondents brought before us the great conflict between Germany and France! What a romantic achievement, worthy to be sung in heroic verse, was the finding of Livingstone by Stanley! Yet, with your contempt for newspapers, you would lose all this profitable entertainment, and seek, instead of it, the accounts of former epochs, written, in most cases, by men in libraries, who had not

PIAZZA DEL DUOMO—COURT OF DIOCLETIAN'S PALACE.

seen the sovereigns they wrote about, nor talked with the people whose condition they attempted to describe. You have a respect for these accounts because they are printed in books, and bound in leather, and entitled "history," whilst you despise the direct observation of a man like Erdan, because he is only a journalist, and his letters are published in a newspaper.'"

"Did Hamerton write that?" asked Lady Saunters. "Does *he* praise newspaper men and — and *Americans* in that way?"

"He certainly does, and" — looking at a card which a servant handed him — "you shall have the opportunity of judging of Mr. Osborne for yourself, for here he is."

"And he *is* our Mr. Osborne! I was sure of it!" Sallie exclaimed delightedly, frankly giving the journalist her hand. "Dear Lady Saunters, he wrote some of those very letters to English papers, relative to the siege of Paris, which Mr. Hamerton praises so highly."

Lady Saunters received the correspondent graciously, and on the next morning the party embarked on a small steamer for the Dalmatian coast at precisely the same hour that Captain Müller excitedly sprang upon the Vienna train. We cannot say that Sallie had no self-accusing or half-regretful thoughts as she watched the prow of the steamer cutting the blue Adriatic, but she was a girl who was accustomed to keep a strong rein upon her own feelings. "I am not going to break my heart for the sake of the captain," she kept saying resolutely to herself, as she listened smilingly and replied intelligently to Mr. Osborne's explanations of the state of affairs in the Turkish provinces and his descriptions of points on the coast.

Their first stop on their second day was at Spalatro, famed for the ruins of Diocletian's villa. Fergusson, in his "History of Architecture," says that this is the only Roman palace of which sufficient remains are left to enable us to judge of its extent or arrangements, and that it gives us a most exalted idea of what the splendor of the imperial palace at Rome must have been, when we find one emperor — neither the richest nor the most powerful — building for his retirement a villa surpassing in size, as it did in magnificence, most of the modern palaces of Europe.

"I wonder whether he was happy here," Sallie asked, as they threaded their way between the Corinthian capitals.

"I think we need not envy him," James Osborne replied, "for he was old and sick in body. Do you not notice that the two principal apartments in the villa are a temple to Æsculapius and his own mausoleum? It seems to say that he had built the temple to the deity of the physicians as a last hope, but with very little certainty of his recovery."

"Poor Diocletian!" Sallie murmured. They were pacing the long and splendid gallery which extends along the entire seaward side of the palace. "What a magnificent view we have from this arcade, and its being placed here shows that the emperor must have appreciated its beauty. How often he must have walked to and fro here, looking away to Italy!"

Lady Saunters condescended to be interested, and asked her husband why the ruins had not long since been carried to London and set up in the South Kensington Museum.

"Do arrange for it, my dear. I am sure they are a great deal more interesting than those broken-nosed things which Lord Elgin brought back."

"Unfortunately, the Austrian Government might have something to say if in this instance I joined the Société pour le Vol des Monumens Anciens," Lord Saunters replied good-naturedly.

Their next landing-place was Ragusa, for here Mr. Osborne wished to meet Peco Pavlovitch, a leader of the Montenegrins, who had sallied out to the assistance of the insurgent Herzegovinians, and was encamped in the neighboring mountains. He urged Lord Saunters to accompany him, saying that he felt sure that personal observation would change his views of what he persisted in calling "the bandits."

RAGUSA.

As Gus snuffed adventure in this expedition, he was eager to join at, and was allowed to do so. The gentlemen set off on horseback, accompanied by a guide. It was hard for Sallie to remain behind at the hotel; but, as Lady Saunters insisted that the trip was a very unsuitable one for ladies, she contented herself with remaining at the hotel. Lord Saunters's private secretary, a Mr. Norcross, was left behind to guard them. Mr. Norcross occupied a singular position, evidently regarded as a little more than servant and less than equal; he was treated with the more kindness on that account. He was the son of an officer, and had been a classmate of Algernon Saunters at the military school. He felt keenly his poverty, and Algernon pitied rather than liked him, for, though a brilliant scholar, his disposition was envious and unlovable. They had similar tastes, however, in many respects; and as Norcross hoped for an appointment in the India service, he had applied himself to the study of several Oriental languages, which Algernon had taken up for love of the literature. They were now studying Turkish together. Norcross had great facility in the acquisition of languages, and, it seemed to

MR. NORCROSS.

Sallie, equal facility in the acceptance of other people's opinions: he boasted that he had no religion of his own, that he could become a Buddhist or a Mahometan without violating his own principles. Algernon insisted that his friend did not mean half he said, but Sallie disliked and distrusted the man. Algernon himself was a doubtful quantity in Sallie's judgment. He had shown that he was capable of enthusiasm, and she felt that if only some great cause would appeal to his slumbering energies he might wake up, and do good and noble work in the world for the right. But his inertness exasperated her more than Norcross's assumption of bad principles. "I want a man to be *something*," she said to Gus, "and Algernon Saunters is lukewarm in everything."

"I like him, though," Gus insisted. "There's stuff in him which will show itself yet, only you are such an awfully impatient 'hitch-your-wagon-to-a-star' kind of a girl. But I tell you what, Sallie, don't have anything to do with that Norcross,—he's a cad."

After the departure of the gentlemen, Sallie persuaded her chaperon to go with her to the citadel, to see the refugees from the districts invaded by the Turkish army. Mr. Norcross accompanied them in this expedition. Lady Saunters liked the young man because of a certain superficial resemblance which he bore her son, which had struck her at their first meeting; and when Norcross had failed to receive the appointment which he had hoped for, she joined with her son in persuading Lord Saunters to engage him as his secretary.

They found the refugees in the greatest of destitution. The Austrian Government issued rations amounting to about half enough food to support life, and they were dependent for the remainder upon private charity.

Lady Saunters, while entirely disapproving of the refugees, handed Mr. Norcross her purse, and commissioned him to distribute loaves of bread among them.

"Why don't the silly things go back to their homes?" she asked of the secretary.

"Because, madam, they are afraid of the Turks."

"But the Turks will not hurt them if they are not insurgents. Is there any one among them who can speak English? I would like to have a good talk with them."

Mr. Norcross replied that there was one family, in another part of the fortress, whose daughters could speak a little English, for they had attended a mission school. As they approached them, Sallie was struck with their well-to-do appearance, in strong contrast with that of the other refugees. The two sisters, Marika and Katarinka, were strikingly unlike. Marika's broad white forehead was as pure as a pond-lily; her eyes were blue and shy; she was dressed in a white

PEASANT GIRLS.

robe with belt at the waist with two great clasps of burnished silver, and necklace of silver coins, and a strand of gold beads was her only other ornament; her whole appearance was full of simplicity and modesty. Katarinka, her elder sister, had a more decided but less pleasing countenance. There was a vindictive look in the slant glances of her dark eyes, and her rich lips had a sullen turn. She was more showily dressed than Marika, with a profusion of sequin necklaces and other jewelry. Both of the girls held skeins of yarn of their own spinning, Marika a hen, and Katarinka a basket of pomegranates, which they offered for sale. Their father scowled sullenly in the background, and the mother tended a sick child.

"You are from the interior?" Sallie asked; "and they tell me you have attended an American school."

The faces of both girls lightened instantly, and Katarinka replied,—

"Yes, lady, at Samokov."

"Ah! then you must know my friend, Alice Newton."

Marika knelt quickly and kissed Sallie's hand.

"Why are you not at the school now?" Lady Saunters asked sternly.

"We live in Servia, half-way between Ragusa and Samokov, and were at home on vacation when the Turks under Mukhtar invaded our country, and we fled here for protection."

"You would have done much better to put yourself under the care of the American missionaries at Samokov," Lady Saunters replied authoritatively, "and Mukhtar Pacha would respect them, while now, by running away, you put yourselves in the attitude of conspirators. I advise you to go straight to your school, and not to bother your heads about the war. It will soon be over. My husband represents England, and he has gone to advise Peco Pavlovitch to lead his disorderly bandits back to Montenegro; and as soon as he does that, and the Turks find there is no army in the field to fight, why, of course, there will be no fighting."

The girls looked very doubtful. "Cousin Trajan says we will never have a settled peace until we have a war," Marika replied. "He says that, if all the provinces united, they could drive the Turks out; and his opinion is held by all 'Young Bulgaria.' It was cousin Trajan who advised us to come to Ragusa, for he says that we are going to have terrible times, and that even the missionaries will not be able to protect us; but here we are under Austria and near Montenegro. Cousin Trajan says the only two men capable of saving the Christians are Prince Milan of Servia and Prince Nicholas of Montenegro. If they will only combine and set the example to the other states by declaring war against Turkey, Bulgaria and the rest will rise, and we will not need the assistance of any of the great powers of Europe to settle our affairs. Cousin Trajan has gone to Belgrade to see Prince Milan, and he is going to see Prince Nicholas too" —

"Sh!" said Katarinka warningly; and Lady Saunters exclaimed that she feared cousin Trajan must be a very bad man, and a traitor and conspirator.

"You will never make Marika think so," said the older sister. "She is betrothed to Trajan. He is a jeweller of Tatar Bazardjik in Bulgaria. He made all our jewelry. Marika is not fond of trinkets, so she gives most of his presents to me. Only the buckles to her girdle she would not give to any one, for they represent her betrothal. See, one clasp is engraved with Trajan's initials, and one with hers; and, while those clasps hold together, the engagement holds."

"It is a very pretty fancy," said Sallie, examining the buckle. "Your cousin Trajan must be a very clever goldsmith. I should think he would be sorry to have you so far away. I really think that you would be as safe at the mission-school, and that you had better go back. I will write a note for you to take to my friend, Miss Newton. You must tell her that I am coming to see her, and that I hope to find you both at the school."

Sallie purchased the girl's yarn, and Lady Saunters made them each a small present, reiterating her assurance that there would be no war in Bulgaria or Servia, for the Herzegovinian outbreak would be speedily put down.

"Those are the first Bulgarian or Servian girls that I have seen," said Mr. Norcross. "If they are all as pretty, I don't blame the Turks for wishing to keep their provinces."

CHAPTER VI.

THE ADVENTURES BEGIN.

WHILE the ladies were having this interview, the gentlemen of the party pursued their way over a rocky, mountainous road toward the camp of the insurgents. Sometimes the track wound around the cliffs close to the sea, and they had superb views of the Adriatic and its islands; then, again, it plunged into a dark defile, or climbed the steep mountains winding toward the interior.

It was nearly nightfall when, jaded and weary, they reached a pass overlooking the camp, a collection of miserable huts. Several armed men, dressed very much like stage bandits at the theatre, in a profusion of gold embroidery, velvet jackets, baggy trousers, leggins, and fez caps, with a most formidable array of long rifles, pistols, and daggers, stopped their progress.

Mr. Osborne handed one of them a paper, which was signed by their leader, and the man volunteered to show them to the hut of Peco Pavlovitch.

Wild-looking men started up on every side, and Gus, more than half frightened, rode close to Mr. Osborne.

"Are you sure that you have not made a mistake, and that we have not fallen into the hands of the Turks?" he asked.

"Certainly," replied Mr. Osborne, "these men are all Christians. You can tell that by their mustaches: Turks wear full beards, while Christians in this country shave all but the upper lip."

"Well, here is a jolly go!" Gus exclaimed: "by that rule, Lord Saunters is a Turk of the worst kind."

"You are possibly not far wrong in your deductions," Mr.

CORRESPONDENTS ON THEIR WAY TO PECO PAVLOVITCH'S CAMP.

Osborne replied, in a low voice, and subsequent events proved that the Englishman's beard was not regarded with favor by the insurgents. The leader, however, received them all courteously, and a rude but appetizing supper of roasted kid was immediately served them, after which they were invited to a council in Peco's hut.

The room was filled with smoke, and, though Algernon could make out a word now and then, neither Gus nor Lord Saunters could understand what was said; but it was interesting to watch the faces, some of them seamed with ugly scars, some fierce and revengeful, others, as it seemed to the boy, very fine and noble.

Gus especially liked the heroic appearance of the Herzegovinian voivoda, or leader, Ljubibratic. Peco seemed to him more sad than savage. He wore a vest of silver mail, and Turkish weapons damascened with gold. Among them was a cimeter of Damascus, which had been taken from some fallen Turkish officer. He sat silently through the greater part of the council, listening to the remarks of the other chiefs, and to those of a Russian gentleman, who seemed, like themselves, to be visiting the camp, but upon whom Lord Saunters looked with great *hauteur* and suspicion.

THE WAR CORRESPONDENT.

After the council, they were shown to a hut, which was placed at the disposal of the guests. Lord Saunters, thoroughly wearied, retired at once, and was soon snoring loudly. Mr. Osborne opened his knapsack writing-desk, and began writing a newspaper letter by the light of a candle stuck in a bottle. Gus watched him until late into the night, as he wrote sheet after sheet, throwing them on the floor by his side as he finished them. The candle sputtered and fell, and still he wrote, wrote, — supplying its place by another which he took from his pocket. The Russian sat by the rude fireplace, smoking, and chatting in a low voice with Algernon and with a handsome stranger in a black turban. Gus, with an eye toward the sensational, at first wondered if he were not a Turkish spy, in spite of the fact that he wore the distinctive mustache. They were evidently talking about the war, for the stranger drew a map in the ashes on the hearth, and Gus heard the names of Prince Milan and Prince Nicholas, and the word Bulgaria, frequently repeated. At last, the Russian rose, knocked the ashes out of his pipe, and, shaking hands warmly with the stranger, retired. The man in the black turban still sat answering Algernon's questions and watching Mr. Osborne as he wrote; and Gus was very sleepy now, — his eyes seemed dancing sparks, which winked and glimmered, and finally went out in the darkness.

When he awoke, it was broad daylight, and Mr. Osborne, who possibly had not been to bed at all, was shaking him, saying that it was time to have breakfast, and begin their return journey.

The stranger, who, Mr. Osborne explained, was a travelling goldsmith, would accompany them, as he had said that he wished to catch the Austrian Lloyds steamer, and go on without delay to Montenegro. So he was not a spy or a Turk, after all, but only a prosaic pedler who had possibly sold Peco Pavlovitch his beautiful silver cuirass, and, no doubt, found the trinket-loving chiefs good patrons of his wares.

Peco came to see them at their breakfast, and talked warmly with Mr. Osborne, but appeared to regard Lord Saunters and his son with some mistrust. The latter said to Mr. Osborne, "Ask him how it is that he, a general under Prince Nicholas, who has not declared war against the Turks, is here with the insurgent Herzegovinians."

Mr. Osborne translated his reply. Peco stated that, so far from sympathizing with the Herzegovinians, Prince Nicholas had sent him

COUNCIL OF WAR AT PECO PAVLOVITCH'S CAMP.

out to dissuade their voivoda from insurrection. Ljubibratic would not listen to him, and Peco, greatly enraged, arrested him, and was carrying him back to Montenegro a prisoner. But on the way the voivoda argued his own cause so eloquently that Peco was won over, and, liberating his prisoner, returned with him as his ally.

Lord Saunters expressed his disapproval of this conduct in strong terms, but this Mr. Osborne did not see fit to translate, and, bidding farewell to their host, they were soon on their return to Ragusa.

But their adventures were not at an end. They were within an hour's ride of Ragusa when their guide pointed out to them the Turkish fort of Czarino, which commands the highway from Austria to Herzegovina. "The insurgents would like to take that fort," he said, "but the Turks are too strongly intrenched for them. However, they are only prisoners in their own fortress, for the Herzegovinians watch them as a cat watches a rat-hole, and not a turbaned rat of them dares venture out. There is a party now in ambush at the next turn, waiting for some unwary Turk to venture this way."

Algernon Saunters did not like the look of the ambuscade, and asked if there were not some other road to Ragusa; but Mr. Osborne laughed at his fears, and approached the party fearlessly. What was his surprise when the leader allowed all to pass except Lord Saunters, insisting that he must remain with them!

"I told you so!" groaned his Lordship. "They are brigands, and they intend to hold me for ransom."

Mr. Osborne and Algernon remonstrated, and showed the passport signed by Peco. "That is all very well for you," replied the guard, "but this man has no passport, and we believe him to be a Turk."

"A Turk!" exclaimed the newspaper correspondent. "Any one can see that he is an Englishman!"

"That makes no difference. The Englishmen are all Mohammedans, and support everything that Turkey does."

"But this gentleman is not a Mohammedan. He is a Christian, like yourself."

"If he is a Christian, why does he wear a beard?"

"It is the custom in England."

"We do not believe it. If the gentleman will shave off his beard, we will allow him to pass on. If not, he must remain in our custody."

Mr. Osborne explained the conditions. "But I have left my shaving-case at Ragusa," demurred Lord Saunters. "That is of no consequence. I will shave you," replied one of the insurgents.

Algernon started, and his hand flew to his revolver. "It is a scheme to cut my father's throat in cold

A BARBAROUS OPERATION.

blood," he whispered to Mr. Osborne. "If there is any shaving to be done, I will do it," he said, aloud. The insurgents did not understand his words as well as his movement. One of them threw a scarf over his body, and strapped his arms tightly to his side.

"There is nothing for it but to submit," explained Mr. Osborne.

INSURGENTS IN AMBUSH.

"I do not think they meditate any evil." It was not, however, without solemn assurances on the part of the insurgents, and not until after much argumentation, that his Lordship yielded his nose to the rude hand of the mountaineer, and his chin to a dull razor. He turned very pale as the cold steel touched his throat; and it was really a severe trial of nerve. It was not until the ordeal was over, Algernon unbound, and considerable distance had been placed between them and the ungentle barbers, that any of the party recovered their spirits sufficiently to joke. "I consider that a very barbarous operation!" exclaimed his Lordship, not at all intending a pun, as, mourning the departed glories of his whiskers, he regarded his lacerated countenance in a little hand-mirror. "I'm sure, I don't know what my wife will say. I believe she married me for my whiskers."

DEPARTED GLORIES.

Lady Saunters was, indeed, very angry. She wished her husband to make a memorial of his disfigurement, and send it at once to the English Parliament and to the King of Austria. It was not until her husband had promised that he would "think of it" that she was at all appeased.

They were to leave Ragusa that evening, and Sallie visited the citadel to give Marika her note to Alice.

She found the girl looking very happy. There was a stranger

with the family, whom she presented as "Cousin Trajan." He bowed politely, but speedily withdrew; not, however, before Sallie had scrutinized him closely. He wore a long, red, fur-trimmed cloak, frogged across the breast, like the coat of an army officer. His face was somewhat sad, but singularly refined.

"Cousin Trajan says," chatted Marika, "that he thinks we may return to Bulgaria. There will be no fighting at present, and, when there is, we are to go up into the Balkans, to the village of Batak, where his mother lives, and there the Turks will never find us. His father owns a saw-mill, and he can employ my father in lumbering, and it is only thirty miles from Tatar Bazardjik, where Trajan's shop is, so that he can come to see us often. So to-morrow we return, and Katarinka will go for the present to the mission school at Samokov. But if war breaks out we will take Miss Newton with us to the Balkans, and you must come and visit us there in the hot weather."

"May I come too?" asked Mr. Norcross, who had come to the citadel with the bread sent by Lady Saunters; but Marika shrank back timidly, and made no reply, while Katarinka scowled scornfully at the presumptuous stranger.

CHAPTER VII.

MONTENEGRO.

ON leaving Ragusa, the travelling jeweller came on board the steamer. Gus pointed him out to his sister, and told of the circumstances of their first meeting, and how he had imagined him a spy. It happened that the man turned his face toward them while they were speaking of him, and Sallie caught her brother's arm with the whispered exclamation, "Why, it is cousin Trajan!"

"What do you mean?" asked Gus, and Sallie in turn told her story. She had hardly finished, when Algernon Saunters brought the jeweller forward, and presented him as Trajan Evanova, explaining that he was on his way to Montenegro with some curious filigree jewelry for Prince Nicholas. At their request, he showed his wares to the party, and Sallie bought a necklace of coins, and Lord Saunters a nearly globular bull's-eye watch. "That watch is Bulgarian," said Mr. Osborne: "I have seen some exactly similar made by the native goldsmiths of Monastir."

The merchant gave the correspondent a significant look as he replied, "The goldsmiths of the different provinces frequently interchange their work and their ideas."

They found the man courteous and intelligent. Algernon had taken a great fancy to him, and he often chatted with them, Mr. Osborne acting as interpreter. He told them of the system of taxes which grinds down the poor peasants, who pay four-fifths of what they produce to the Porte. "The silks of Turkey are justly noted," he said, "but see how can they be manufactured when the government taxes

COUSIN TRAJAN.

every mulberry tree, the land upon which it is grown, the silk-worms that feed upon it, the raw silk, every yard of goods, and even the labor of the weaver. If the poor man has no money to pay his taxes, the officer seizes his manufactured goods, his loom, his household furniture. If he objects to this, he is beaten and imprisoned.

"It is so with my own industry. Not a foot of land can be owned in the provinces by any one but the Sultan. The owners of the gold and silver mines pay fully four-fifths of their products for the privilege of working them, and I must be bled in like manner for every conceivable item of my stock in trade."

Mr. Evanova acknowledged to Algernon, in confidence, that

MONTENEGRIN SENATOR.

he was a Bulgarian, and the young man suspected that his errand with Prince Nicholas was a political one.

Cettinje, the capital of Montenegro, is situated at a day's journey from the coast, and is approached either from the port of Cattaro, where there is an excellent hotel, or from Spitza. As the latter route would give them a trip across the Lake of Scutari, besides taking them through a more picturesque region, and as Lady Saunters was a good horsewoman, and both she and Sallie preferred making the excursion to Cettinje to being left at a seaside hotel, the party did not land again until they reached Spitza, where they were taken over the mountains, in a sort of rude jaunting-car, to the Lake of Scutari, across which a boatman took them, in a small sail-boat, to the heart of Montenegro.

The mountains were all around them, gloomy and sombre; and Sallie remarked to Algernon Saunters that she did not wonder that the little country had been named the Black Mountains, or that the Turks had been unable in four hundred years to wrest it from the hardy mountaineers, while they had conquered all the other provinces with the exception of Dalmatia, which is under the protection of Austria.

Algernon entered at once into an animated conversation on the subject of the Turkish principalities. "If they had only remained united," he insisted, "these provinces of Bosnia, Herzegovina, Dalmatia, and Montenegro, as they were under the Romans, they might have formed a powerful nation, which could have easily maintained itself against the Turks on the one hand and the Russians on the other. They preferred to remain distinct; Bosnia ruled by kings, Herzegovina by dukes, and Montenegro by vladikas, or prince bishops, until 1851, when the prince gave up the ecclesiastical dignity."

The party had left Lake Scutari, having landed at the little town of Riska, where they were to engage horses to take them to Cettinje.

Mr. Norcross reminded Algernon that he had expressed a desire to visit the monastery of Ostrog, not far from Rieka, in order to examine its library, and Lord Saunters also announced that he would like to see this famous old monastery. As no accommodations could probably be obtained at the convent for ladies, Mr. Norcross proposed to obtain a guide at Rieka, and to escort the party to Cettinje, leaving Lord Saunters and Algernon to spend the night at Ostrog. This plan did not appear to suit the usually acquiescent Algernon.

"I think I had better go on with mother," he said. "You, Norcross, can rummage in the library for me, and make notes of anything which you think will interest me. I do not think I care to make the acquaintance of those musty old monks."

It was accordingly decided that Lord Saunters and his secretary should remain at the monastery until the next day, and the rest of the party proceeded to Cettinje.

"For what is the convent so celebrated?" Sallie asked of Algernon as they rode side by side.

"It was a seat of learning in the Middle Ages," the young man replied. "In 1492 there was a printing-press established here, before the art of printing was in general use elsewhere. The press was used until 1852, when, during a Turkish invasion, the types were melted into bullets."

Their ponies were sure-footed as chamois, and, though the bridle-path was execrable, the ride was not so dangerous as it seemed.

"One can hardly believe," said Algernon, "that this is the main thoroughfare to the capital. Why does not Prince Nicholas construct a better highway?"

"The answer is very simple," replied the goldsmith. "Prince Nicholas is not so disinterested as to open the way for Turkish artillery and other military trains into his country. These rocks are his fortress, and he has need of them, for yonder is a Turkish fort, just across the border."

Their Montenegrin guide, who trudged sturdily beside their horses, sneered at this remark, and, laying his hand upon his yataghan, remarked,

MONTENEGRIN SCENES.

"The Turks will not cross the frontier, they dare not, they know that we would be only too glad to see them."

What a picturesque fellow this mountaineer was, in his white tunic embroidered in gold, his dark blue Turkish trousers laced below the knee with bright braid, a round cap of varied colors, and his belt an entire armory of pistols and daggers! Lady Saunters declared that he was a bandit leading them away to a mountain fastness.

"If that is the case," said Sallie, "I shall have a chance to sketch, for I have brought my water-colors with me."

"I do not believe," said Lady Saunters, "that any one, with the exception of my husband, Algernon, and myself, will be detained. The only object of these brigands is ransom, and they have a very keen eye as to where it can be obtained. That explains the safety with which Mr. Osborne can travel among them: he has nothing for them to steal."

"If that were the case," Gus replied, "why didn't they rob the jeweller when Lord Saunters was shaved? He had his case of goods with him, and they knew it; and there was that Russian gentleman, — he had a very wealthy look. I believe he is some prince travelling for pleasure. I saw a jewelled decoration on his breast when his overcoat was thrown back, and yet none of Peco's men offered to molest him. Besides, they didn't rob Lord Saunters, or say a word about money, and this man has a very honest look. I don't think we need be afraid of him."

Just as Lady Saunters's fears were becoming unappeasable, the little cavalcade reached Cettinje. They found the capital of Montenegro a straggling village on two streets, which unite, forming a letter T. The houses were small white cottages for the most part; while the government building, containing the senate chamber, the arsenal, the printing-office, etc., was of very modest dimensions. Prince Nicholas's palace was a plain, one-story edifice, and the monastery was the only picturesque building in the town.

Mr. Osborne domiciled them in a pleasant inn. Algernon joined them at table after a short tour of exploration about the town.

"It is a charming place, mother," he remarked. "Why not decide to stay here for a week? Osborne, Evanova, and I have arranged a horseback trip. We start to-night and may not return for a day or two."

He spoke cheerily, — almost, Sallie thought, with forced gayety. Lady Saunters, without noticing this, was not pleased.

"I would rather you would put off this trip, Algernon," she said, "until your father returns. I do not think that he would approve of your leaving Miss Benton and me with no protector. Suppose something should happen — that the Turks should fall upon this town, and Mr. Norcross away too; none of us speak Arabic or Hindoostanee, or any of those outlandish tongues. We could not even tell them that we are English."

A shade crossed Algernon Saunters's face; he was deeply annoyed, but he concealed his vexation. "Master Benton, here, is studying Greek," he said, "and Miss Benton speaks French perfectly — besides, dear mother, you are perfectly safe in Cettinje. I am quite sure that my father would approve of my plan."

"Say no more about it, Algy," Lady Saunters replied, in the same tone in which she had been accustomed to deny him sweets when he was a boy in knickerbockers. "I really cannot spare you in the absence of your father. You will make me very wretched if you persist in your self-will."

"You are quite right, Lady Saunters," said Mr. Osborne. "Your son's duty at this time is at your side."

Algernon gave him a strange look, and seemed about to speak; but as his mother rose from the table he offered her his arm, and led her dutifully from the dining-room. Sallie was about to follow, but Gus detained her.

"You will let me go, will you not, Sallie? You won't baby me the way Lady Saunters does that great, grown man, — will you, dear?"

MONTENEGRIN SOLDIER.

Sallie glanced inquiringly at Mr. Osborne, who replied quickly, "I can't take you this time, Gus. You had better remain with your sister. You will know why by and by." His tone piqued Sallie's curiosity, but she made no inquiry. Gus strolled out-of-doors, and she was mounting the stairs when she met Algernon Saunters coming down in haste. "Stop a moment, Miss Benton," he said. "Has Mr. Osborne gone? I must see him."

The war correspondent came forward as he spoke. "We may as well take Miss Benton into our confidence," said Algernon. "I cannot remain behind, I must go with you."

"Let Miss Benton be the judge of that," replied Mr. Osborne. "The matter is, that I have just learned that a party of Montenegrins leave Cettinje this evening for Rieka, as they have heard that a night attack has been planned by the Turks on the fortress-convent of Ostrog. I have thought best to accompany the Montenegrins to look after Lord Saunters, and this young man desires, very naturally but very foolishly, to accompany me. He will not be of the slightest use, and, on the other hand, may be needed here. It is not necessary to alarm Lady Saunters by putting the case before her; she has decided it very well without knowing all the interests at stake. If Lord Saunters should fall into the hands of the Turks, his son's presence would be vitally necessary to his mother."

"And, on the other hand," Algernon broke in excitedly, "you can understand, Miss Benton, that no one with the feelings of a man could allow a rescuing party to go out in search of his father without accompanying it."

"I understand," replied Sallie, "and I sympathize with you,— but do you really promise to abide by my decision?"

"I will," replied Algernon, "for I am so torn by conflicting opinions that I do not know what to do."

"Are you certain," Sallie asked of James Osborne, "that he can do no good by accompanying you?"

"Absolutely certain of it," the correspondent replied.

"Then," said Sallie, "I think your duty is with your mother." Algernon turned impatiently on his heel, and strode out of the hotel. James Osborne smiled. "He is not over-polite, Miss Sallie," he said, "but never mind, you have advised him rightly. Do not worry about us unless we fail to put in appearance by to-morrow evening, in which case you had better lay the matter before Prince Nicholas."

PRINCE NICHOLAS.

Sallie was intensely anxious, but she succeeded in disguising her feelings, and in giving her Ladyship a pleasant evening. Lady Saunters imagined that her son had given up his excursion entirely out of deference to her authority, and was extremely gracious. Algernon was unusually silent, but as they parted for the night he contrived to say to Sallie, "You were quite right; pardon my boorishness."

The next morning they spent in strolling about the town, and in the afternoon Lady Saunters insisted that they should make a call of ceremony upon Princess Milene. They were surprised to find here the Russian gentleman whom Algernon and Gus had met at the insurgent camp.

He was introduced to them as Mr. Ignatieff, and it was explained that he was in no way related to the prince of that name, but was a simple editor of a Moscow journal. Gus could not help thinking that he did not look at all like a literary man, but that his bearing was decidedly military. There was no stoop in the shoulders to betray bondage to the desk, but they were thrown back in a way that told of habitual horseback exercise.

While the Russian gentleman conversed with the Prince, the ladies chatted with the Princess. She had a gentle manner, but her face indicated great firmness and intelligence, and the complicated affairs of the little country had been left in her hands and well managed during her husband's absences from Montenegro. Lady Saunters complimented her on the admirable *finesse*

PRINCESS MILENE.

shown by the Prince in not allowing himself to be drawn by his subjects into a declaration of war with Turkey.

The countenance of the Princess fell. "If you knew how very difficult it is not to declare war," she said, "to hold back our high-spirited chiefs, and tamely to submit to the degradation of looking on while the

Turks are butchering our brethren! Ah! nothing but the fact that such a step would be the suicide of the nation keeps him in this attitude of policy. It is useless for Montenegro, single-handed, to become the champion of Christendom as long as such powerful nations as England and Russia, by their indifference, encourage the Turks to oppress, rob, and maltreat their Christian subjects in every conceivable way."

MR. IGNATIEFF.

Mr. Ignatieff had overheard her remark, for he turned and replied in a low voice. "Russia is not so indifferent as you think. I have heard that Prince Milan of Servia has entered into negotiations with the Czar, which may lead to developments which will create considerable surprise among the Great Powers."

An eager light came into the Princess's eyes. "If this were only true!" she said.

"Madam!" exclaimed Lady Saunters, "you surely cannot wish to see this peninsula plunged into the horrors of war."

"A disgraceful and criminal peace is still more horrible," replied the Princess.

"Milene!" said the Prince warningly. "My dear madam," he continued, addressing Lady Saunters, "be assured that I will endeavor, so far as lies in my power, to maintain the peace of Europe; but I am not an autocrat. I can keep the nation back as a nation from declaring war against Turkey, but I have no power over my subjects as individuals; and the greater part of our fighting force is now in Herzegovina, engaged, every man on his own responsibility, in fighting the Turks, who in their turn do not scruple when they dare to make raids upon my territory. It is fortunate for your husband, madam, that I was informed of their intended attack on Ostrog, and sent out a force to defend the fortress yesterday."

MONTENEGRINS.

It was the first intimation that Lady Saunters had had of her husband's danger, and she was much alarmed. The Prince re-assured her partially by explaining that the forces must have arrived at Ostrog, and the Turks have been informed of their arrival before the time set for the attack.

"There will be no fighting," said the Prince. "The Turks are cowards. It was all very well to massacre a few defenceless priests, but as soon as they know that the monks are not the only men in the convent, the rich plunder in Ostrog will not seem so desirable."

"If England has so much influence in Turkish affairs," suggested Sallie, "why does she not restrain Turkey from making her rule in her European provinces so oppressive?"

"England doubtless could do this if she would," the Prince replied.

"And England shall!" Algernon Saunters exclaimed with much warmth. "The Sultan shall be made to understand that the great heart of the English people will not allow him to mismanage his affairs and bully his subjects in this shameless fashion. I had no idea — English people generally have no idea — of the extent of taxation and oppression which you have just explained to me. I intend to investigate the matter still further, and devote what influence I possess to insisting on a speedy reform."

"I am sure," murmured Lady Saunters, "that my husband will report what we have heard, on our return to England, to his friend Lord Beaconsfield. I have no doubt everything can be amicably arranged if Prince Nicholas can maintain his admirable peace policy a little longer, and Prince Milan will not allow Servia to rush into war trusting to the deceitful promises of support from wily Russia."

As Lady Saunters said this, she threw a glance of scorn toward Mr. Ignatieff, who maintained an inscrutable expression of countenance.

Lady Saunters returned to the inn secure in her supreme confidence in Lord Beaconsfield's ability to regulate the affairs of Europe by his peace policy; but as the hours dragged slowly by, and it was now long past the time that Mr. Osborne had said they might be expected, Algernon became intensely anxious. He paced the veranda, listening acutely from time to time for the clatter of hoofs which should proclaim the safe return of his father and friends. Sallie sat with Lady Saunters, and listened politely to her gentle flow of amiable chat, until she ended in bidding her a calm good-night. Algernon was sitting in an attitude of dejection on the veranda, and Sallie stole quietly out to him. She pointed to a group of men who were standing under a large tree in the centre of the village. They seemed to be engaged in earnest debate, and Sallie asked if this was not the tree under which the chiefs were accustomed to hold their councils of war.

The council, if such it was, broke up presently, and one of the men, who wore a long red cloak, crossed the square, and entered the palace; and Sallie felt sure from his gait that it was Prince Nicholas. Another, whose carriage had something in it which was familiar, approached the inn, and Algernon, who could restrain himself no longer, asked if any news had been received from Ostrog. "I was just coming to inform you," replied a voice, which Sallie recognized as that of Mr. Ignatieff, "that a courier has returned from Ostrog, and no attack has been made. Your friends are, in all probability, quite safe."

"Thank you," Algernon replied warmly, "and yet is it not strange that they do not return?"

"They may be waiting for an escort; and, even if they should fall into the hands of the Turks, Lord Saunters, as an Englishman, would not run the danger which a man of another nationality — a Russian, for instance — might encounter."

"Do you think that Mr. Osborne and his companion would be roughly handled if captured?"

"I would not like to be in their shoes; but Mr. Osborne is a representative of America, and a non-combatant, and they are both under the protection of Lord Saunters. Besides, we know nothing to lead us to suppose that they have been captured. It is, however, no time to travel in European Turkey, and I would advise the ladies especially to leave the country."

"Mr. Ignatieff," asked Sallie, "is there going to be a general war? I have particular reasons for knowing, and I believe you can tell me. Will Russia espouse the cause of the Turkish provinces?"

"I am not prepared to say what Russia will do as a nation, but if the Czar does not take a stand in behalf of these people, who belong to the same great Slavic race with ourselves, and are Christians like ourselves, I have no hesitation in saying that a large proportion of the Russian officers will offer their services to Prince Milan of Servia. However, this is hardly the time or place for a discussion of the Eastern question. Pray be assured that your friends are in no immediate danger, and consider me entirely at your service should you have need of me at any time."

With a profound bow the Russian withdrew. Algernon drew a long breath of relief. "I have been trying to think," he said, "that if I have suffered so much mental torture from the thought that my father, who is backed by the English nation, may be in the power of the Turks, what must be the condition of mind of these poor beggars of Bulgarians."

"I think it is time that somebody thought about them," Sallie replied simply.

"We are all so selfish," Algernon replied hotly, "we think only of what concerns ourselves."

"That is putting it rather strongly," said Sallie. "Say rather that these people are so far away that we do not realize their troubles."

She turned to go in, but he called to her: "Miss Benton, I want to thank you now while I have the opportunity."

"For what?" she asked, much surprised.

"For giving me an object of interest. You have waked me up,

and now I intend to look after these poor people a little. Perhaps I shall be able to do something for them; perhaps in striving to do this I shall amount to something myself. If I do, it will all be your fault. Do you understand?"

"No; but I am very glad. Good-night."

CHAPTER VIII.

LORD SAUNTERS IS TAKEN PRISONER.

AFTER leaving their friends, Lord Saunters and Mr. Norcross proceeded in the direction of the convent of Ostrog. They rode leisurely, and, as it was still early in the afternoon, they turned aside from the regular route to explore a bridle-path which led into a grove of chestnuts. They had not ridden far when two men sprang from the ground and seized Lord Saunters's bridle, while another dragged Mr. Norcross from the saddle. It needed but a glance at their captors to tell them that these were no Montenegrins. They were darker and more brutal men, and they wore the Zouave costume.

Lord Saunters knew at once that he had fallen into the hands of Mukhtar Pacha's advance-guard. The men conversed together in Turkish, while his Lordship produced his passport, and protested loudly that he was an Englishman. Mr. Norcross aired the little Turkish which he knew, and insisted on being taken to their commanding officer.

The men partly understood him, and evidently regarded him of more importance than his Lordship, whom they fastened to a tree, having first emptied his pockets. The soldier in command of the squad took possession of these effects, and informed Mr. Norcross that his request was about to be granted, and that he was to be taken immediately to headquarters. After a little further parley, he persuaded the man to allow him first to speak with Lord Saunters, and to give him the use of writing materials. "I will do the best I can," he assured his employer, "but these Turks are rapacious creatures, and you will doubtless have to pay a heavy ransom."

His Lordship, thoroughly terrified, handed Mr. Norcross his letter of credit, and made out a blank check payable at Constantinople to the bearer. "Don't peril our lives, Norcross, by trying to save me money," he said. "Fill it out for whatever sum the bandits demand, and get us out of this predicament as soon as possible."

"Trust to me," the secretary replied, and at the time he had no intention of proving unfaithful. He was escorted through the wood, down a rocky defile, to the Turkish camp, and presented at once to the commander, who addressed him after examining the passport.

A TURKISH COMMANDER.

"I understand," he said, "that we have the honor of holding as prisoners two English gentlemen of rank. I presume that I address the son of Lord Saunters?"

It was a characteristic of Mr. Norcross that he did not scruple at a falsehood; he assumed boldly the character assigned him, and assured the general that, under the existing friendly relations between their governments, he was at a loss to understand upon what pretext two English noblemen were thus detained. The Turk stroked his beard softly, and looked at him from the corners of his slant eyes. He was evidently studying his man. "Tell me," he said, "the purpose of your journey, and your plans."

Mr. Norcross mapped out their proposed route.

"All this, you say, is for pleasure," said the general. "Pleasure should not be the chief object in life of a young man like yourself. You should have a career. You have spoken of the friendly relations existing between our countries. The Sultan recognizes them, and is willing to assign high posts in our army and navy to Englishmen of birth and ability. You have had a military education. How would you like to put it in practice? We are on the eve of a war of more importance

BASHI-BAZOUKS.

than this paltry outbreak — a war which will give opportunities of distinction and advancement. Will you join us?"

Mr. Norcross felt that he was completely in the man's power, and he answered, with many protestations of delight and friendship, that a commission in the Turkish army had been the dream of his youth. He admitted, however, that his father might object to this arrangement, and that it was not at all convenient for him to remain with him at present, but if the gentlemen would kindly allow him to depart, and arrange his affairs, he would give his word of honor to report himself at Constantinople as soon as possible.

The general smiled incredulously, gave him another sidelong glance, and then turned aside to receive some reports which had just come.

"You will accompany us for a short distance," he said finally, to Mr. Norcross. "I have just learned that Ostrog is to be re-enforced; we will accordingly fall back. Do not be alarmed, you will be released in a few days."

All that night the division was on the march, and at daybreak it joined the main army. Here Mr. Norcross found Lord Saunters, who had been treated much more roughly than himself. After a short interval of rest, the tents were again folded, and the army continued its retreat. Division after division marched away, but the squad who guarded the Englishmen remained in their places until an orderly rode up, and handed Norcross a sealed package. "The general bids me say to you," he said in Turkish, "that, if you hold to your purpose of going to Constantinople, you may find it to your advantage to present this to the Minister of War. You are now free to go where you will."

The aid galloped away, the guards cut the cords which bound the prisoners, and hurriedly fell into the ranks of the last column, and they were left standing by the side of the road. Mr. Norcross placed the packet carefully in his breast-pocket, and turned to Lord Saunters, who was nearly exhausted with fright and fatigue.

"We are free," he said, "and we had best make our way to Ostrog with all speed, before we fall into the hands of stragglers." Not exactly sure of their way, they wandered about that day to little purpose in the mountains, but were fortunate enough to find themselves at the door of a hut belonging to a goat-herd, where they received food and shelter. Here Lord Saunters took heart and courage a little. "We have had a wonderful escape," he said. "Why, Norcross, after you left me, the scouts brought in another prisoner, a Montenegrin, and hanged him right there before my eyes. I suppose I owe my escape to you. How much did you have to pay the general? I shall not grudge a thousand pounds if we only get safely out of this beastly country."

The Turkish general had not suggested the payment of ransom, and Lord Saunters's draft still lay in his own pocket. Very subtly the temptation came to him to take advantage of this circumstance, and to trust to being in Constantinople at some future day to claim the money for his own use. He replied that he had made out the draft for twelve hundred pounds, quieting his uneasy conscience as he did so with the reflection that the money was not yet stolen, and that he need not take it if he should think better of the project. Lord Saunters expressed himself as satisfied. He had not noticed the delivery of the packet to Mr. Norcross by the Turkish aid, and his only feeling was one of profound gratitude for his escape. The goat-herd guided them in the direction of Ostrog. When in sight of the convent, they were again frightened by the approach of a small company of horse, and gave themselves up for lost until they recognized Mr. Osborne at their head, and understood that this was a party which had come out in search of them. They were taken to the convent, kindly cared for by the monks, and the next morning proceeded to Cettinje, Lord Saunters's ideas of the Eastern question materially changed by his captivity. He had seen such acts of violence, and had been in such mortal terror and danger, that he was not proud of England's *protégés*. He had an interview

PORTICO OF A COTTAGE IN MONTENEGRO.

with Prince Nicholas, and assured Sallie thereafter that his opinion in regard to the Turks had greatly altered.

"They are too blasted insolent, you know," he said, as they left Cettinje for Cattaro. "The Prince tells me that they have impoverished their provinces by taxes which the poor people haven't the money to pay, and that they have let loose upon them a lot of Circassian beggars, who have swarmed over Bulgaria, driving the poor Bulgarians out of their homes, and occupying them without so much as saying, 'By your leave.' Then, there are a lot of other grievances, of which Mr. Evanova tells me, enough to convince me that the matter ought to be looked into."

"I am glad to hear you say so, father," said Algernon. "Mr. Osborne has invited me to make a tour with him through Bulgaria, and I should like to avail myself of this opportunity."

"That is hardly practicable, certainly not just now," replied Lord Saunters. "You know we have made an appointment to meet the Prince of Wales at Athens. But I shall certainly run up to Constantinople after our interview with the Prince, and see our ambassador, Sir Henry Elliot, and sift this matter thoroughly."

MR. NORCROSS LOOKED UP.

Mr. Norcross looked up at the mention of Constantinople, and seemed about to speak. He evidently thought better of it on consideration, for he said nothing.

"If you have determined to go to Constantinople," suggested Mr. Osborne, "and Miss Benton and her brother desire to visit Miss Newton at Samokov, it will be altogether the best plan for them to travel with you. There is a railroad from Constantinople to Philippopolis, and at the American Mission at Constantinople a suitable escort can be easily obtained to the mission at Samokov."

Algernon Saunters brought forward a convincing argument in the suggestion that if Miss Benton put off her visit to her missionary friend until after seeing the Davenports, Turkish affairs might become so complicated that it would be impossible for her to make it at all.

Every one united in urging Sallie to continue her journey with the Saunterses, and she finally agreed to do so, writing Melicent that she would use all her powers of persuasion to induce Alice to leave the country with her, and that her visit was not given up, but simply postponed.

From Cettinje the party proceeded in company to the seaport of Cattaro. Their first glimpse of the city as it lay beneath them, the red roofs and white walls of its beautiful villas relieved by rich foliage, was one of enchanting loveliness.

Here they bade good-by to Mr. Osborne and to Mr. Evanova. "I shall hope to see you again before long at Samokov," said the correspondent.

"And in the mean time I wish you would send letters also to 'The London Trimmer,'" said Algernon Saunters. "It is a paper which always sides with our party, and it has taken too light a view of this business. I will write to the editor, recommending you."

"Should you see Alice before I do," was Sallie's last word at parting, "do advise her for the best, and not let her run any danger by remaining in the country if there is to be trouble."

Trajan Evanova heard this message. "I shall also see Miss Newton soon," he remarked, "and I will look carefully to her safety. No harm can come to her at my parents' home in the mountains, and that is open to her if she chooses to remain in Bulgaria and take her chances with the people she has come to help."

"I think I would rather she would leave the country," Sallie replied.

"But I thank you heartily for your hospitable offer. We will decide when I visit her next month."

Thus it happened that Sallie's plans were completely changed, and that, instead of speeding toward Vienna, to the friends who were so impatiently expecting her, this beautiful autumn day found her taking the steamer at Cattaro for Athens, *via* the Ionian Isles.

CHAPTER IX.

MELICENT AND CAPTAIN MÜLLER.

AND all this time what of Sallie's good knight?
It had been a great disappointment to Captain Müller not to find Sallie on the Vienna train. How eagerly he scanned his fellow-passengers at the station, and when the train stopped he walked up and down the platform in the vain hope of discovering her in one of the compartments. He came to the natural conclusion that she had missed the train, and he determined to stop at Perchtoldsdorf and take the next express for Vienna, sure that he would find her upon it. He strolled into the old church, and listened to its history of blood and fire: for it was here in 1683 that the citizens took refuge from the Turks, and from the church, having been promised mercy, they marched out to a frightful massacre, over thirty-eight hundred butchered in cold blood. He grew angry as he listened, and on his way to the station he purchased a paper in which he read of the probability that such scenes were soon to be repeated.

"I wish Germany would take a hand in driving the Turks into Asia," he said to himself. "I should like to enlist for such a crusade." And then he thought of Sallie and her fixed disapprobation of war. "I wonder how she thinks those fellows are to be managed, anyway," he thought, and then the train came in, and he began another fruitless search for Sallie, and finally sprang on board, much dejected by her absence. So confident had he been of finding her that he had not asked the address of her friends, Mrs. and Miss Davenport. He reflected, however, that they could easily be found through the police,

CHURCH OF PERCHTOLDSDORF.

and, before going to his hotel, he left an inquiry at the proper office, a natural enough proceeding on his part, but one which was destined to give the ladies some annoyance in future.

A Russian detective happened to be at the bureau. He had come to Vienna to trace a Nihilist, Natocha Melniketzky. There was something in the description which Captain Müller gave of Melicent Davenport which attracted his attention. "Melicent,—Melniketz!" he murmured to himself, "the disguise is very thin!" and his beads of eyes twinkled with malicious exultation. The captain noticed him only as an unusually homely man, with phenomenally large ears. Later on, the Davenports were to have the honor of a more intimate acquaintance.

A RUSSIAN POLICE AGENT.

As far as concerned the captain's immediate purpose, interviewing the police was the best thing which he could have done, and an official speedily sent him the address for which he was in search.

The Davenports had not yet received Sallie's letter explaining her change of plans, and were consequently in daily expectation of her arrival.

Captain Müller was much cheered, and, to pass away the intervening time, proposed an excursion to the *château* of Eisgrub, the most beautiful of the ninety-nine different residences of Prince Lichtenstein.

The day was a charming one, and they spent it in rambling through the great orangery and the hot-houses with their nine hundred orange-trees and their fifteen hundred aloes, and about the superb park, said to be the finest in Austria, coming upon many surprises in landscape-gardening and picturesque buildings: a mosque with minarets, a pagoda, an artificial ruined castle, a fisherman's cottage, Greek temples and statues, triumphal arches, an aviary and a menagerie, lakes with boats, parterres of brilliant flowers, and beautiful views.

Mrs. Davenport rested in a little temple to the Muses while Melicent and the captain visited the dairy; and neither of them could have told,

CASTLE OF EISGRUB.

on their return, whether the Prince von Lichtenstein preferred Jerseys to Devons, for the captain embraced the opportunity to unburden his heart and seek Melicent's sympathy and advice. He was sure of both, for had she not sheltered and protected him when he was a spy in Paris? And where is the generous-hearted girl who does not take an interest in a friend's love-affair, especially when she is herself happily betrothed! Melicent thoroughly appreciated the blessedness which had come into her own life with the devotion of James Osborne, and she could not understand how any woman could be content without just such a true and noble affection. She was, therefore, delighted to hear the captain confess his interest in Sallie.

"I am sure she loves you!" she exclaimed impulsively, and then, realizing from the great light in the captain's face that she was encouraging him far more than she had any warrant to do, she modified her assertion: "That is, I am sure she will love you. She always took a very great interest in you, in those old days in France. Why didn't you propose to her at Versailles?"

"I did."

"And she rejected you?" — Melicent looked aghast. "Did she give any reason?"

"She said she could never marry a soldier."

"I don't wonder, after all the horrible things she had seen. And didn't you love her enough to change your profession?"

MELICENT.

"I did not think that I did. I did not know then how much I loved her; besides, there was nothing else for me to do. But now" —

"Now you are willing to give up the army?"

"And now perhaps it is too late."

"Oh, I think not! Sallie is not engaged to any one else, or she would have told me. I believe she has waited for you all this time. She would have married long ago if she had not cared for some one. She is a very attractive girl, you know."

"I know it," with a groan.

"Well, she has come to Europe again, and you have another opportunity."

"Do you think so?" exclaimed the captain, delighted; and he took Melicent's hand, and pressed it with such enthusiasm that some people who were passing remarked that it was evident those young persons must be very much in love with one another.

Captain Müller lived on the hope which Melicent extended to him for several days. He was placidly blissful, until the arrival of the

THE DANUBE AT LINZ.

letter which announced Sallie's intention of visiting Alice before joining the Davenports. This plunged him into an abyss of despair. "This does not look much as if she had come to Europe to give me a second opportunity," he said gloomily.

Melicent looked at him in surprise and indignation. "I never said that!" she exclaimed. "I said she had come, *and* you have your opportunity,— if you have pluck enough to make it, I meant. Such a girl as Sallie must be sought. But it is all right: you will have time to get your discharge from the army. Mamma and I intend to spend the winter in St. Petersburg, where I am to study medicine. I do not know how much I shall practise it in after-life, but if war breaks out anywhere, mamma and I will join the Red Cross. Now, Sallie says she intends to stay with Alice only long enough to induce her to leave the country, and that then she will bring her to us. So you have only to break your connection with the German army, and repair to your sister's at St. Petersburg, and you will find Sallie with us, and all will be well."

"And, after I have thrown up my career, what if I find that it is all a mistake, and she does not care for me?"

"If you are so coldly calculating as all that, it might be safer to write her first, and bargain about it: your epaulets for her heart; but if I were Sallie, I should feel much more complimented to feel that you had risked everything, ' to win or lose it all.'"

Shortly after this, Mrs. Davenport and Melicent removed their residence to St. Petersburg. Captain Müller accompanied them on their journey as far as Linz, for Mrs. Davenport had chosen a slightly circuitous route, in order that they might enjoy the views on the noblest part of the Danube.

As the steamer ploughed its way up the river in the moonlight of a superb night, a string-band in the saloon played the Ländler's Waltz, and Melicent sang softly a well-worn song, which somehow lost all its association with itinerant musicians, and although it was October, and not June, seemed very appropriate to that perfect night:—

> "Can I forget that night in June
>   Upon the Danube River?
> We listened to the Ländler's tune,
>   And watched the moonbeams quiver.
> I oft since then have watched the moon,
>   But never, love, ah, never, never
> Can I forget that night in June
>   Upon the Danube River," etc.

> "The boat kept measure with its oars;
> The music rose in snatches
> From peasants dancing on the shores
> In distant songs and catches.
> I know not why that Ländler rang
> Through all my soul, but never
> Can I forget that night in June
> Upon the Danube River," etc.

There was another song which had pleasant associations for Captain Müller, — a little folk-melody, with the refrain, —

> "When I come, when I come, when I come to thee again."

And now the Ländler's took its place beside it.

At Linz the captain bade farewell to the Davenports, and returned to his home, to write the letter which was to disturb the even current of Sallie's life, while Mrs. Davenport and Melicent turned their faces northward. There was a sharp little man, with a wrinkled face and large ears, who looked over Melicent's shoulder as she bought the tickets. His keen eye caught the destination, St. Petersburg. "Ah-ha!" he said to himself, "it was very 'cute in you to take this round-about way. No one less up to your tricks than I would have imagined, when you left Vienna for Linz, that you were going to Russia; but I am on your track, my beauty, I am on your track. You are so fond of travelling, I wonder now how you would like to take a trip to Siberia?"

CHAPTER X.

GREECE.

"OLD friends are best," Lord Saunters happened to remark carelessly, one day. Sallie had not forgotten her old friend. The effort to put Captain Müller entirely from her thoughts was more than even her resolute will could accomplish. But she never faltered: she never spoke of him, or drooped or languished after the approved fashion of love-lorn maidens. She interested herself in the absorbing questions of the day, and grew more and more absorbed in the problem of Turkish occupation of the European provinces. She talked over the matter a great deal with Algernon Saunters, and invented many peaceful solutions of the difficulty, whose adoption, he said, would have done honor to a council of nations, and he regretted sincerely that there was no probability of an advance of civilization during their lifetime sufficient to carry them out. They read a great deal of Oriental literature together, Mr. Norcross joining them in this recreation, for he had a very clever trick of turning Persian sonnets into English verse. "Norcross, you should have been an Oriental," Algernon said one day, "you are so thoroughly steeped with their spirit. Give us again the war-song of the Ottomans."

"It is not my own translation," Mr. Norcross replied; "it was rendered into English by a Mr. Homes, a compatriot of yours, Miss Benton." As Mr. Norcross repeated the vehement lines, a fierce, untamed spirit seemed to glow in his eyes, and the listeners knew that for the moment he made the sentiment his own.

> "'All our hopes and cares are for our country;
> With our own bodies will we form her ramparts.
> We are Ottomans! A bloody shroud
> Shall be our robe of glory.
> Refrain: We march our every step in battle,
> Shouting the profession of our faith.[1]
> We are Ottomans! We sacrifice our lives,
> And we secure Paradise and glory.
>
> On our waving standard see the bloody sword!
> Soul-fear enters not our mountains or our plains;
> In every hill and vale a lion crouches,
> Watching over every acre of our soil.
> Refrain: We march our every step, etc.
>
> Let the cannon roar. Let the iron hail
> Open the gates of Paradise to our brave comrades.
> What have we found in this world
> That we should fear to die?
> Refrain: We march our every step in battle,'" etc.

"Is it not grand?" Algernon asked.

"It seems unutterably sad to me," Sallie replied, "that last line, 'What have we found in this world,' with its implication that we have found nothing for which we care to live. No Christian could feel so."

"The utter hopelessness of Orientalism has often struck me" Algernon replied. "Do you remember how Omar Khayyam speaks of life?

> "''Tis but a tent, where takes his one day's rest
> A sultan to the realm of Death address.
> The sultan rises, and the dark *farash*
> Strikes, and prepares it for another guest.
> A moment's halt, a momentary taste
> Of being from the well amid the waste,
> And lo! the phantom caravan has reached
> The nothing it set out from. Oh, make haste!'"

---

[1] *La Allah ill allah ue Mohammed ressoul Allah.* — "No god but God, Mohammed prophet of God." — *From* "*The Gospel in all Lands.*"

"I see the necessity of making haste," said Sallie; "but I take exception to the assertion that everything begins and ends in nothing."

"It seems very likely to me," replied Mr. Norcross, "and I object most decidedly to making haste. I would rather drift forever with the tide, as we seem to be doing to-day, careless whither it leads me."

October's perfect weather calmed the sea to glass as the steamer left the Adriatic, and skirted the western coast of Albania and Greece.

"The Albanians are many of them Mussulmans, are they not?" Gus asked.

"Yes, indeed," Sallie replied. "Do you not remember Lord Byron's lines?

> "'Land of Albania! let me bend mine eyes
> On thee, thou rugged nurse of savage men!
> The Cross descends, thy minarets arise,
> And the pale Crescent sparkles in the glen.'"

"The Suliotes live just over there," said Lord Saunters. "When I was a young man, I thought there was no martial poetry so stirring as Byron's 'Song of the Suliote,' and, really, it is quite appropriate to-day.

> "'Oh, who is more brave than a dark Suliote,
> In his snowy camis and his shaggy capote?
> To the wolf and the vulture he leaves his wild flock,
> And descends to the plain, like the stream from the rock.
>
> I talk not of mercy; I talk not of fear:
> He neither must know who would serve the Vizier.
> Since the days of the Prophet the Crescent ne'er saw
> A chief ever glorious like Ali Pashaw.
>
> Dark Mukhtar, his son, to the Danube is sped;
> Let the yellow-haired Giaours[1] view his horse-tail with dread.
> When his Delhis come dashing in blood o'er the banks,
> How few shall escape from the Muscovite ranks!'"

On they glided past the beautiful Ionian Isles. One by one they sighted Corfu, Santa Maura, Ithaca, and Cephalonia. The steamer

---

[1] Russian infidels.

stopped at Patras, but did not enter the Gulf of Corinth, much to the disappointment of the young people, who had hoped to visit the ruins of that once beautiful and pleasure-loving city.

IONIC AND CORINTHIAN COLUMNS.

"There is very little left to interest you," Lord Saunters assured them.

"I should like to find and sketch there just one Corinthian capital," Sallie said. "That is such a beautiful legend of how the Greek architect found the acanthus springing through the basket, its graceful leaves, repressed by the tile on the top, curling downward, and so suggesting to him the idea of the most beautiful of the architectural orders."

"I doubt," replied Lord Saunters, "whether there is a single Corinthian capital left in Corinth. I believe there are seven Doric pillars, however."

"Now, what I would like," said Gus, "would be to explore the old race-course, the site of the famous Isthmian games. I would not ask to pick up any columns or capitals — a horseshoe would suit me, and would make a very good relic."

"You can visit Corinth very easily from Athens, if you like," Lord Saunters explained. "A steamer runs down from the Piræus to Kalamaki in about three hours, then you can take a carriage to the Acro-Corinthus, the old citadel, from which one of the finest views in all Greece is obtainable, and return to Athens the same day."

"I have always thought of Corinth as being on the west coast of Greece," Gus remarked; "but of course the isthmus is so narrow that she had the advantage of traffic on both seas."

"Lechæum was the ancient port on the west, and Kenchrea to the east," replied Lord Saunters. "The best way to visit the coast of

Greece is in one's own private yacht; then one can go where he pleases, and stay as long as the fancy takes him, and he is always sure of having good accommodations for the night. I think I shall make such a trip one of these days, and if you young people are on the Continent, I invite you to accompany us. Would you like to do so?"

"Just wouldn't I!" exclaimed Gus, while Sallie expressed her appreciation more gracefully.

SPORTS OF ANCIENT GREECE.

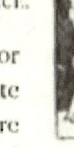

"Then," said Lord Saunters, "we must plan for it for another summer. Ithaca, over there, is said to be quite interesting. They show you the castle of Ulysses, where Penelope waited during her husband's absence. Read the 'Odyssey' this winter, for it is the best guide-book to the island. In Byron's time, and a little later, it used to be quite the fashionable thing for Englishmen to do the Isles of Greece. Lord Houghton has written some clever poems on them. But, with all their charms, England has little cause to love this insignificant chain of islands. They have changed owners oftener and caused their masters more vexation than any bit of country of the same area in Europe."

Gus pricked up his ears, and his Lordship continued.

"In 1797 the Venetians gave up their possession of them to France. Then Russia, Turkey, France, and Great Britain each took a turn in owning them, and in snatching them from one another, until 1815, when they were formed into a republic, under the protection of Great Britain. We did everything we could for the improvement of the country — laid out a hundred thousand pounds *per annum* upon it. But the ungrateful islanders wanted none of our protection, and were continually giving us all the trouble they could. In 1858 Mr. Gladstone was sent out to see what was the cause of all this row, and he soon ascertained that nothing would suit the beggars but complete independence from Great Britain, and annexation to Greece. In 1863 the election of the son of the King of Denmark, the brother of Alexandra, as King of Greece, under the name of George I., gave England a chance to get rid of her unprofitable possessions, and they were turned over to Greece as a sort of good-will offering, wedding present, or that sort of thing, in 1864."

"England's colonies do not seem to have generally appreciated her efforts in their behalf," Gus remarked dryly.

"And yet," Sallie added quickly, "there is no question but that wherever her flag has waved civilization has followed."

Every headland and island, every port or distant mountain, which they now passed bore some classic name. As they rounded the rugged points of Peloponnesus, they recalled the wanderings of Ulysses, while his faithful Penelope worked in Ithaca at her tapestry.

PENELOPE.

And now they were nearing the Cyclades, or *circling* islands, so named because they were supposed to have circled around Delos, where Diana and Apollo were born. And now they have passed Milo, where the most beautiful and noblest of the statues of Venus was discovered; and at last they have reached Poros, the naval station of the kingdom, at the entrance of the Gulf of Ægina.

All the way they have been passing and meeting flocks of sailing-vessels and small steamers, the merchant marine of Greece, plying between the islands and the principal cities of not only the Mediterranean, but of Western Europe. Here they pass a ship bearing the Russian flag, laden with Vino Santo, or Santorin, which the Russians love so well, from the volcanic island of Thera; here is Malmsey for

England, from Tenos; marble chimney-pieces, and other carvings, on their way to France; with Zante currants, honey from Hymettus, olive-oil, figs, silk, and sponges, for Leghorn, Trieste, Palermo, Smyrna, and Constantinople.

Gus had been so much impressed by all this display of shipping that he had expected to see a considerable navy, and was much surprised when told that nearly all the men-of-war in the harbor were English ships, which had gathered to greet the Prince of Wales, the navy of Greece consisting only of one ironclad, six screw-steamers, four schooners, two cutters, and the royal yacht.

"Why, it is almost as bad," the boy exclaimed, "as our American navy!"

"I am proud of the fact that our navy is so insignificant!" Sallie exclaimed. "It proves that the United States has the respect of the other powers, and does not need to bully them."

At the Piræus, the port of Athens, they saw the *Serapis*, which had just arrived with the Prince of Wales, and witnessed his meeting with

IN DOUBT.

the King of Greece, who came alongside in his royal yacht. They had the further honor of proceeding to Athens by the same train with their Royal Highnesses, and, as Lord and Lady Saunters were acquainted with the Prince, Sallie was presented in her simple gray travelling-dress.

The Prince greeted Algernon Saunters most cordially, and repeated the invitation which had already been extended, to accompany him to India.

Algernon, while making suitable acknowledgments for the favor shown, feared that it would not be possible to accept; but Lord Saunters drowned his son's remonstrance with effusive and grateful acquiescence. "What do you mean, sir," he asked his son, a few hours later, "by cutting yourself out of such a magnificent opportunity? Have you forgotten that this is precisely the object for which we have made this journey? Have you forgotten that you are a second son, and have your career to make?"

"I might join the Prince at Bombay, if you insist upon it," Algernon replied; "but I would really very much like to accompany you to Constantinople. I am so much interested in this question of the independence of the Turkish principalities!"

"Stuff and nonsense!" replied Lord Saunters irascibly. "I will look into the matter as far as is necessary, though I assure you that my main object in visiting Constantinople is to forbid payment on that check which was extorted from me under circumstances which amount to simple theft. It is all very well to have exalted ideas of humanity, and all that, but one must look after one's own interests as well. Go out with the Prince, and, if you have a fancy for taking a tour through Turkey, do so on your way home."

"Give me two days to consider the matter," Algernon replied, with a grave and troubled expression.

A few hours more, and the party were domiciled at the Hôtel d'Angleterre, in Athens. Modern Athens is not in itself a picturesque city, but the Acropolis still towers above it, crowned by its magnificent ruins, chief of which is the Parthenon.

Gus had been "cramming" Fergusson's admirable work on architecture during the voyage, and he had learned that the Parthenon is built entirely of white marble, and is the finest example of the Doric style extant. That it was designed for the place which it occupies in so skilful a manner that, while the lines of the pillars appear perfectly straight, to obtain this effect they are in reality constructed in accurate curves to counteract the illusions of perspective.

Sallie had already decided that she must make a sketch of the beautiful little temple (the Erectheum), whose portico is supported by

MODERN ATHENS, FROM THE ACROPOLIS.

columns of female figures called Caryatides. Sallie's sketch-book was already filling with Greek coiffures and jewelry and the honeysuckle ornament, a conventional design, adapted from the buds of the honeysuckle.

Gus, thinking of the story of the origin of the Corinthian, the honeysuckle ornament, and other vegetable forms, was planning an essay on " Botany in Architecture ; " but Lord Saunters advised him to wait for this, until he had an opportunity to study mediæval Gothic and the Renaissance.

Both of the young people were eager to set out at once for the Acropolis ; but Lord Saunters, referring to the daily newspaper, found an announcement that there would be a grand illumination of the Acropolis

CARYATIDES.

that evening, in honor of the Prince ; that the fireworks would be superb, and it might be well to obtain their first impressions of the place from this unusual spectacle.

How odd it seemed to be reading the daily newspaper in Neo-Hellenic, a language differing very slightly from classical Greek ! Sallie could read it without difficulty, and Gus found it easier than Homer. " I shall get Tricoupi's History of the Greek Revolution," Sallie announced, " and begin to read it here."

"Do, my dear," advised Lady Saunters. " I think it will do for our Friday readings."

" I am afraid we may find it too exciting." Sallie replied. " You know it describes the struggle with the Turks, and their final victory in 1820, when, by the countenance of the European powers, they were able to establish an independent kingdom."

" And there are some Pallikars, or Braves," said Algernon Saunters, looking from the hotel window. " You know that when Thessaly was ceded to the Turks, these people left their homes, and migrated to Southern Greece rather than remain under Turkish domination."

Gus looked out, and saw a group of wiry, fierce-looking men, wearing red caps, white shirts, and heavy gold-embroidered jackets, with very full white kilts. They were armed to the teeth, and were followed by servants loaded down by more weapons.

"These men would like nothing better," said Algernon, "than to have a general war, which would give them license to fall upon the Turk. England will have to keep a fleet in the Piræus to preserve peace."

"Oh, let them fight it out!" Gus exclaimed. "It seems to me this peace policy, which only serves to keep the weaker party from defending itself against bullies, is getting to be rather a chestnut."

Sallie was horrified, and expected to see Gus sternly rebuked; but, to her astonishment, Algernon Saunters only smiled.

The *fête* in the evening proved to be a very brilliant one, and Sallie was delighted that her visit to Athens had chanced to fall upon such an exceptional time. The party rode out to the Acropolis in open carriages, and watched the fairy-like effect. First, the grand mass of ruins, outlined vaguely against the starlit sky; the waiting crowd, standing in expectant hush; then the flash of the Bengal lights, and the noble pillars, with all their matchless symmetry, were brought into strong relief against the strong shadows.

"It is wonderful! it is wonderful!" Sallie exclaimed, enthusiastically, and even Lord Saunters admitted that "it capped any similar show" he had ever seen. Only Lady Saunters was dissatisfied. "The temples are so frightfully out of repair," she complained: "not at all kept up, like our Houses of Parliament, my dear."

Sallie was charmed with the little Temple of the Wingless Victory, the delicacy and grace of whose Ionic columns, with their curling ram's-horn capitals, contrasted with fine effect with the Titanic strength of the Doric pillars of the Parthenon.

THE PARTHENON.

"I understand," she said simply, as she rode homeward with Algernon and her brother, "the meaning and beauty of the promise, ' Him that overcometh will I make a pillar in the temple of my God.'"

"I have changed my mind about that essay," Gus remarked. "I

THE TEMPLE OF THE WINGLESS VICTORY.

shall lay aside 'Vegetable Forms in Architecture,' and write on 'Pillars,' — the Doric, the Ionic, the Corinthian, and the Caryatides, which, I suppose, illustrate best that idea of our being pillars in the church."

"It seems to me," Algernon said curtly, "that most of us are only pilasters."

"I do not quite understand," said Sallie.

"Gus is enough of an architect to explain the difference between a pilaster and a pillar," Algernon replied.

"I catch on," Gus exclaimed irreverently. "A pilaster is sometimes only an ornamental pillar, fastened to the wall, apparently aiding in the support of the temple, but not necessary to its construction."

"I am afraid most of us are little more," said Algernon, who was dissatisfied with himself. "I am strongly tempted," he continued, "to give up my proposed trip to India, and to return to England *via* the Turkish provinces, prosecuting in this way the investigations which I have begun."

He was not thoroughly selfish, and he had been strongly stirred by what he had seen and heard. His English sense of justice was outraged by the mismanagement and oppression exercised by Turkish rule. "What would you advise me to do?" he asked. "I am ashamed and indignant that England should support such outrages."

"Then, why don't you collect the facts, and lay them before the English public?"

"That is just it. I am afraid that I shall become a fanatic, and go back to England howling for reform." The young man became uneasy under Sallie's quiet, steady gaze. It was impossible not to be entirely frank, with those eyes reading his soul. "And then, after all, it's none of my business, you know, and I am not quite ready to throw away all my chances in life for the sake of championing the oppressed. If I go out to India with the Prince, I am likely to receive an appointment. I am only a beggar of a second son, you know. There, I've made a clean breast of it all. What do you think of the situation?"

"I think you are in just the position of that rich young man whom Jesus loved, and whom he asked to leave all and follow him. You have position and influence: if you attend to this matter, which appeals to your heart and conscience, you may effect great things for humanity, and find the grand opportunity of your life — that of working with God."

"And do you ask this sacrifice of me?"

"I have no right to ask it. It is not a matter in which I am at all concerned, except as your earnest friend; but I think Christ asks it of you. Still, you must decide it for yourself. Is the demand too great?"

"If, as you say, you are not at all concerned in it, yes, I think it is."

The carriage had stopped before the hotel, and Gus had sprung out. Algernon descended, and extended his hand to assist her to alight. The action was commonplace enough, but there was a look of unspeakable entreaty on his upturned face. A pang of pity shot through Sallie's honest, kindly heart, as she realized for the first time what this meant, and, like the young man in the Scripture to whom she had just referred, they both "went away sorrowful."

AT THE MUSEUM.

It was the last time that she was to see Algernon Saunters for many months, and, although she had not been to blame, the memory of his face was not a pleasant one.

The next day the English division of the party passed in making calls upon their acquaintances, and in driving out to the royal country-seat. Sallie and Gus spent it industriously in the museums, especially interested in the collections made by Dr. Schliemann. In the evening there was a state banquet given by the King and Queen of Greece to the Prince, but, as the young Americans were not invited, they contented themselves with viewing the fireworks in front of the Temple of Jupiter Olympus, and with hearing an account of the banquet from Lady Saunters. On Wednesday the royal festivities closed with a luncheon to the King and Queen of Greece, given by the Prince, on board the *Serapis*. In the evening the royal ship steamed away, with

Algernon Saunters on board. He had left without bidding Sallie good-by, and, to the surprise of Gus, for whom he left a fine set of Greek photographs, without leaving any message for her.

On the next day our party made their proposed excursion to Corinth, accomplishing more in one short day than our space will permit us to chronicle (since our story is not of Greece, but of Turkey and Russia), and on Friday they left the Piræus for Constantinople.

CHAPTER XI.

FIRST IMPRESSIONS OF TURKEY.

AS Sallie sailed up the Bosphorus, and entered the Golden Horn, it seemed to her that she had never seen anything half so beautiful as this first view of Constantinople. The radiant white city stepped down to the sea by a series of terraces; its domes and minarets and glittering palaces rising from gardens and groves of cypress, and shining in the morning sunlight like a vision of the New Jerusalem. The glamour was not entirely dispelled by a nearer view, for, though she caught glimpses of narrow, crooked streets and of much filth and poverty, still even the poorer quarters were extremely picturesque, and they passed many magnificent stone houses, built in the ornate Oriental style of architecture. Chief among these were the Seraglio and the Mosque of St. Sophia. The bazaars, a collection of over six hundred shops, all under one roof, interested Lady Saunters greatly. Each little street was devoted to one particular class of goods: for instance, the niches on one little lane were filled entirely with amber; strings of beads, mouthpieces for pipes, and ornaments of various kinds, all carved from this beautiful substance. Other streets were devoted individually to the display of silks, rugs, scarfs, perfumes, brazen lamps and pitchers, inlaid and painted furniture, pipes, weapons, slippers, embroideries, and a hundred other articles.

But the people themselves were the most interesting of all. Here was a gray-bearded merchant, sitting cross-legged in his bazaar, for all the world like a picture from the "Arabian Nights;" and here was Scheherezade, veiled, with the exception of one coal-black eye; and the donkey-drivers were jostling each other, and the water-carriers bawling, just as she had expected. They were all so interested that they strolled from one street to another, not noticing where they were going, until Lord Saunters suddenly discovered that they had become separated from Mr. Norcross, and that they were lost. He attempted to inquire the way to Pera of a passer-by, but he either did not or would not understand. It was in vain that he reiterated the word "English." A shrugging of the shoulders and a spreading of the palms was the only response. Sallie saw that they were in a more crowded quarter of the city. Presently she was jostled by a Turk with an evil expression, who muttered curses instead of apologies; and a crowd collected, pointing and jeering, while the street boys threw mud and small stones.

Lord Saunters was greatly incensed. "We will see if English tourists are to be insulted on the streets of Constantinople!" he exclaimed, and began to bluster in his haughty way, when an unsavory vegetable hit him squarely in the face. At that instant, a gentleman in the costume of a European sprang from a bazaar, offered his right arm to Lady Saunters and his left to Sallie, and led the party quickly out of the mob, to the underground railroad which connects Constantinople with Pera, its European suburb.

"These are unsettled times," he remarked, "and it is hardly safe for strangers to ramble about this part of the city."

At Pera they seemed suddenly to emerge into a European city, so great was the change from Stamboul, the true Turkish Constantinople Gus remarked on the English and French signs over the shops, the foreign post-offices, the Christian churches, an Italian opera, and a circulating library. They established themselves at the Hôtel d'Angleterre. (Sallie had observed that, no matter where they were, they stopped at the Hôtel d'Angleterre.) His Lordship called immediately at the British Embassy, and reported the disappearance of Mr. Norcross.

He was told that there was probably no cause for alarm: that he

SKETCHES AT CONSTANTINOPLE.

, doubtless, simply lost his way in the crowd, and would soon find
.n. He received, on the other hand, very little encouragement in
ard to the ransom which had been
rted from him. Diplomatic business
much involved, and there seemed to
no possibility of laying the matter
ore the Sultan. He might call on
bankers, and leave orders to refuse
payment of the check when pre-
ted; but this seemed to Lord Saun-
hardly an honorable thing to do.
He returned to the hotel, depressed
irritable.

LORD SAUNTERS DEPRESSED.

"I shall go to the American Mission to-morrow." he said to Sallie,
I see whether I can procure proper escort for you to your friends.
If not, I strongly advise your not attempt-
ing the journey."

The visit to the American Mission
proved more interesting than they had
anticipated, and here Sallie found a letter
awaiting her from Alice. It was a long,
enthusiastic letter, full of delight at the
coming of her friend. Alice did not believe that there was serious danger, certainly not for foreigners, and she would
count the days until Sallie's arrival. A
Mr. Humphrey would leave Constantinople
soon, on his return to Philippopolis. He
was an earnest missionary, just the one to
take charge of them; and she had written requesting him to conduct
the young people on their journey.

GUS'S IDEA OF MR. HUMPHREY.

Gus was not over-pleased with this prospect. He insisted that Mr.

Humphrey would prove to be a disagreeable, priggish, and sanctimonious old fraud; and he drew such an amusing portrait of Mr. Humphrey, as he imagined him, that Sallie was convulsed. "He will think it wicked to drink cider, I know," said Gus, "because it works on Sunday. And here's good-by to every speck of fun for the rest of the trip."

"We will see." Sallie replied hopefully. "I, for one, am so thankful that on this Sunday we can attend a Christian church, and hear the dear old, familiar hymns!" The day was passed quietly. They attended services at the American Mission. Before entering the church, they took a lingering view of the beautiful minaretted city, and, as they took their seats, Sallie started to hear Dr. Doddridge's hymn, which seemed to have been written for this very place and hour.

MR. HUMPHREY APPEARS.

> "See Salem's golden spires
> In beauteous prospect rise,
> And flowers of Paradise
> In rich profusion spring;
> The Sun of Glory gilds the path,
> And dear companions sing."

That afternoon, the servant brought in Mr. Humphrey's card. Lady Saunters descended with Sallie, and they were surprised to recognize the gentleman who had rescued them from their unpleasant predicament on their arrival. He had an intellectual face, refined and pleasing manners; he was dressed in quiet, good taste, and he presented in every way the appearance of a man accustomed to the amenities of the best society.

He was courteous, intelligent, and prepossessing. "He is so very nice," Lady Saunters admitted afterward, "that I felt quite sure that it

ENGLISH INSULTED IN CONSTANTINOPLE.

would be improper for you to travel with him, until he told me that he was going out with his wife."

Mr. Humphrey offered to show them over Robert College,—an invitation which was gladly accepted; and Sallie enjoyed the surprise of her brother on meeting the missionary, and finding him so different from what he had imagined.

She was herself surprised at the extent of the college, the beauty of the buildings, and its valuable collections.

Mr. Humphrey gave them an interesting account of the origin of the college. "In 1850, when Mr. Hamlin was American missionary here," said Mr. Humphrey, "his attention was drawn to the fact that, wherever a Turk embraced Christianity, his fellow-Turks instantly boycotted him, declining to give him employment, or patronage of any kind, so that starvation for himself and family stared him in the face. Mr. Hamlin attempted to give employment to these cases, by inventing trades for them, but soon found that there were so many of them that some large business must be maintained to be at all adequate to the demand. He puzzled his brain for some time to light upon something which could not be put down by the Turkish authorities, and, after a good deal of research, discovered that one of the former Sultans, who desired to attract emigration to Constantinople, had issued a *firman* permitting every foreign colony in the city to maintain its own bakery. Now, there was at this time quite a colony of English residents in the city, and no English bakery, while Turkish bread was very poor. Mr. Hamlin called upon the English banker, and explained his project of establishing a steam-bakery. The banker considered the idea a good one, and advanced a sufficient sum for the plant. Mr. Hamlin went right to work, ordered his machinery, and proceeded to experiment in bread-making. He taught his men how to carry on the business, engaged customers for them among the foreign residents, and soon had them doing a paying business.

"Then the Crimean War broke out. The price of flour rose enormously; many of his customers left the city, and a famine broke out among the poor. Mr. Hamlin, in the absence of regular business, turned his bakery into a charitable institution. He had six thousand pounds of coarse Graham flour, not up to the standard of what they had been in the habit of using, but sweet and wholesome, and this he made up into bread, and, with the help of a committee of foreign residents, he distributed among the poor. Then the English army began to arrive, and Lord Raglan engaged Mr. Hamlin to furnish it with bread, a commission which amounted to five thousand loaves a day. When the British army withdrew, it was deemed advisable to close the bread business, and Mr. Hamlin turned over the entire profits, twenty-five thousand dollars, to the American Board, to be used as a church and schoolhouse building fund."

"And that was the way the money was obtained for the founding of Robert College?" Sallie asked.

"Not exactly; but the college owes its existence to Mr. Hamlin's bakery in another way. In 1856, Mr. Robert, a wealthy American, was sailing up the Bosphorus, when a boat laden with bread, bound for the English hospital, passed him. The delicious odor struck him, and he asked where such good bread was made. On learning that it was at the American Mission, he was indignant. 'And this is the way our missionaries fulfil their trust, and go about their business of saving men's souls!' he exclaimed. He called upon Mr. Hamlin, intending to investigate the matter, and to denounce him to the Board. Mr. Hamlin explained everything to him, and, instead of denouncing, he praised. More than this, he became deeply interested in the mission, and gave more than *two hundred thousand dollars* to the establishing of this college."[1]

Sallie was greatly interested in all that she heard and saw. She was introduced to some Bulgarian students, gentlemanly fellows, wear-

---

[1] This account of the origin of Robert College is drawn from "Stories from a Missionary's Note-Book," by Ex-President Cyrus Hamlin, published in *The Golden Rule*.

ing the European costume, and conversing fluently in French and English, and she thought that they compared well with the Harvard and Yale men of her acquaintance. She conversed with one of them on the condition of political affairs in Bulgaria. "We all long for independence," he said, "and the league called 'Young Bulgaria' is looking anxiously for some opportunity to accomplish this end; but I see no possible chance for us, and we will probably be severely punished by the Turkish Government for this feeble desire. A young man of my acquaintance published a volume of Bulgarian poems, and, because he included in it a few old national ballads, he was thrown into prison. Some of the foreign legations made a little talk about it, and, the matter coming to the Sultan's ears, the poet was promptly beheaded, in order to put an end to the agitation."

STUDENT OF ROBERT COLLEGE.

As Lord and Lady Saunters had planned to remain in Constantinople for a few days, Mr. Humphrey kindly offered to show them about the city. Mr. Norcross had not appeared, and the party were becoming very anxious for his safety,—Lord Saunters even feared that he might have been murdered. A visit to the bank on the following day placed an entirely different construction on his disappearance. Lord Saunters's check, filled out, not for twelve hundred, but for four thousand pounds, had been presented and cashed by a European, whose description Lord Saunters immediately recognized as that of his secretary. The evidence was overwhelming. Lord Saunters had been tricked by Mr. Norcross, who had now absconded with the money. Under the existing confusion in Constantinople, there was no way of tracking the scoundrel, and his Lordship bore the loss with more equanimity than might have been expected.

"I shall have the less to leave Algy," he said, with a sorrowful shake of the head.

"And the less with which to do such deeds as Mr. Robert's," Sallie added, apparently not perceiving the startled look in Lord Saunters's face, which told that he had not thought of such a disposal of his funds.

"That is true," he said, after a moment's pause. "What is given away is the only money that is put 'where thieves do not break through.'"

The next day was devoted to excursions by water in a caique to the different environs.

At Scutari they visited the English and Turkish cemeteries. Among the cypresses in the former were buried many of the English who fell during the Crimean War. There was a terrible daily death-rate at the English hospital at Scutari, until Florence Nightingale came out from England with her little band of devoted nurses, and took charge of its wards.

Sallie listened to the story of this heroic woman, not thinking that she would soon be engaged in the same work. In the Turkish cemetery they saw a veiled woman rise from beside a grave, and glide away. The tombs of men here bore the emblem of the turban. Mr. Humphrey pointed out to Gus the tomb of the favorite horse of the Sultan Mahmoud. "I should like to know what he did to merit this distinction. Perhaps he bore his master victoriously through some battle. Did you ever see General Sheridan's horse? You know they have it stuffed at the museum at Governor's Island."

Mr. Humphrey had seen Sheridan's horse, but he could not tell the story of Sultan Mahmoud's, and regretted that no Turkish Browning had written a ballad on its exploits.

That afternoon, Gus, for the first time, experienced the overrated luxury of a Turkish bath. He could not persuade Lord Saunters to accompany him. "I shall not willingly put myself into the hands of these savages," he explained. "I have had enough attention given to my toilet by Montenegrins and Turks."

MONUMENT IN THE BRITISH GRAVEYARD, SCUTARI.

The description which Gus gave of his experience did not cause his Lordship to regret his decision.

"First," said Gus, "I got into swimming costume, then I lay on a couch until, as the little shaver said, 'I was all Presbyterianism.' Then

A FAMILY CORNER — TURKISH CEMETERY, SCUTARI.

the Jack of Spades, who bosses the concern, took me into an oven, laid me down on a hot stone, and kneaded and paddled and thumped and massaged and punched and pummelled and squeezed and wrenched and tortured me generally. Then he dashed on a lot of scalding water, and lathered and skinned me; finally he rigged me out in a toga made of Turkish towelling, and gave me a hookah to smoke. I think he was mad because I wouldn't touch the dirty thing to my lips; but I managed to gulp down the little cup of black coffee he brought, and that seemed to appease him some. I tell you that fellow earned his money: there is more exercise in it than in a game of football. Indeed, I couldn't help thinking, all the time, that it *was* a block game, and that our side was getting awfully beaten. I had such a good chance to tackle that old Blackamoor in the scrimmage, it was all I could do to keep from kicking the sponge right out of his hand, clear over the goal."

Lord and Lady Saunters remained with them but one day more. The day was devoted to a more satisfactory view of the Turkish city, under the guidance of Mr. Humphrey, than their first had been. They visited the palace of the Seraglio, and happened to catch a glimpse of the Sultan Abd-ul-Aziz, as he rode through the city. "His face is more weak than wicked," Sallie said; "I fancy he is afraid of his own subjects." The furtive glance and pale face were distinctly remembered as she read, not a year later, that he had been deposed in favor of Mourad V., and had committed suicide.

ABD-UL-AZIZ.

MOURAD V.

Lord Saunters and Gus, by paying a fee, were allowed to see the interior of the beautiful Mosque of Suleiman the Magnificent, with its six minarets, and that of St. Sophia. The latter is built in the form of

TOMB OF SULTAN MAHMOUD'S FAVORITE HORSE.

a Greek cross, and Gus recalled the fact that it was built by the great Emperor Constantine as a Christian church. They could see the figures of the Cherubim dimly through the whitewash with which they had been covered. Mr. Humphrey pointed out some pillars said to have come from the Temple of Diana at Ephesus.

"The Russians," said he, " and other members of the Greek Church, look longingly toward this church, and dream of the time when it will be restored to the Christian faith."

And this again came back to Gus, as later he heard the marching Cos-

BASHI-BAZOUKS.

sacks singing songs, whose spirit Edna Dean Proctor has rendered in her

"EMPIRE OF THE EAST.

"Hail to the glorious morning,
   When the cross again shall shine
On the summit of St. Sophia,
   O city of Constantine!

In the sky of the South, at midnight,
   We have seen God's flaming sign,
And we know he will drive the Moslem horde
   As chaff from his sacred shrine.
Silent will be the Muezzin,
   As the sun on Asia sets:
Folded the crescent banner,
   Crumbled the minarets.

Then, in the grand cathedral
   Victorious chants we'll raise,
While the saints look down with loving eyes,
   And the gems of the altar blaze.
Hail to the day when the eagles
   And the cross shall gain their own,
As the patriarch welcomes our Lord, the Czar,
   To the Cæsar's ancient throne."

   Sallie and Gus were sorry to bid farewell to their English friends. In spite of their differences of taste and inherited habits of thought and life, the companionship had been very pleasant for all, and a firm friendship had been formed, while the electric sparks of influence which go out from every life like Sallie's had quickened and kindled Lord and Lady Saunters to new considerations of their responsibility.

   On board the steamer which was to carry them homeward a Turkish vessel from the eastern shore of the Black Sea landed its passengers — a regiment of irregular Circassian troops, the terrible Bashi-Bazouks, soon to be turned loose upon Bulgaria, to punish its unformulated desire for independence. The pay of this corps consisted in permission to pillage the unhappy country, and they shortly after accomplished this task with a brutality of wholesale slaughter unsurpassed in the annals of the world's history.

But before this was done Sallie reached Samokov safely, and was warmly greeted by Alice. She found her friend teaching in the girls' school. Marika was here, looking lovelier than ever, and Katarinka was one of the brightest scholars. There were scattered acts of atrocity on the part of the Turks, — twenty Bulgarians were murdered before Christmas, — but there was no general outbreak of war; and at Samokov all was so peaceful that it was difficult to believe that the country was on the eve of a great convulsion. Alice was an enthusiast in her work, and could not be persuaded to leave it. "I will go with you next summer for a little tour during the vacation," she had said to Sallie, "if you will spend the winter with me here."

The idea pleased Sallie. Mr. Osborne was in Samokov, and had offered to take Gus with him on a tour which he proposed to make through Bulgaria and Servia. Sallie was glad to have her brother under the influence of such a man; and, as she noted the picturesque types about her, she felt sure that she could spend a season of art-study very profitably in the companionship of her dearest friend Alice. The cost of living was less here than in any European city, and she settled herself very contentedly at the mission. But she had not calculated on the contagion of Alice's zeal. Sallie very soon discovered that her friend was overworked, and offered to take her class in sewing for her. She became so interested in it that she declined to give it up, and soon assumed another in penmanship, and the sketching became an entirely secondary affair. She caught at the language easily, and soon learned to sing the hymns, and talk brokenly with her pupils. Suddenly, in the midst of this pleasant occupation, there came to her a letter which made her heart leap with a wild, sweet exultation; for with it there was a little packet, from which rolled no gems of price, but Captain Müller's epaulets. He had given up the army for her sake.

CHAPTER XII.

ST. PETERSBURG.

DESPITE the annoyances which were to follow, Melicent's first experiences in St. Petersburg were very pleasant. All was so odd and delightful, so different from any other European city which she had seen.

The railway station was surrounded by droskies, and their drivers, who knew no English, but were adepts in the universal sign-language. Melicent had learned a few Russian phrases, and advanced boldly, holding up before the group which immediately formed about her a coin, and naming the hotel to which she wished to be taken. The brotherhood of drivers received this proposition with scorn. Melicent turned away from them with a magnificent air, and, drawing her mother's arm within her own, walked away. A driver followed her, screaming "*Pojalooyte*," which Melicent took for surrender; and the two ladies mounted into the queer little gig, and were driven rapidly through the Nevsky Prospect, the principal avenue of the city.

The wideness of the streets reminded the two ladies of Washington,

DROSKY-DRIVER.

the city of magnificent distances. All was on a grand scale, spacious and grandiose; here the citizens had evidently room to breathe; private houses had the appearance of palaces; the shops were alive with elegant ladies, making purchases: and generals and noblemen dashed through the street on horseback or in sumptuous carriages. They

ST. ISAAC'S CHURCH.

passed the Admiralty, and turned into St. Isaac's Square, named from the magnificent cathedral which fronts it. Melicent succeeded in stopping her driver, and in entering the building. She found it extremely simple, but impressive from its vastness. Each of its four porches is supported by immense granite pillars, sixty feet in height. The interior carried out the same feeling of immensity. Looking up

BIRD'S-EYE VIEW OF ST. PETERSBURG.

into the great dome, Melicent's brain reeled with wonder at the power of man to accomplish such a result. It was a relief to turn from it to the jewelled shrine of Prince Demidoff, the owner of the malachite

STATUE OF PETER THE GREAT.

mines of Siberia. Melicent was fond of malachite, with its varying shades of exquisite green, and she examined with interest the beautiful specimens of which the dome of this shrine is formed.

"I wonder where we can find articles made from malachite for sale," she said to her mother.

"I fancy we had better wait until we have been here some time," Mrs. Davenport replied. "I have always found it a good plan not to purchase souvenirs until just before one is about to leave. You learn the current prices, and have an opportunity to compare and choose. Very likely, too, Captain Müller's sister can give us points."

In the centre of the great square in front of the cathedral stands the statue of Peter the Great. They had an excellent view of it from every side. St. Petersburg is an extremely flat city, with no rocks in its vicinity, consequently great masses of stone are at a premium; and the Emperor Nicholas selected for the pedestal of this statue a huge bowlder, and caused it to be transported to the city from a great distance. The statue, a very spirited one by Falconet, has a fine, realistic effect. Peter appears to be riding up an eminence, and is just in the act of reigning in his horse on the brink of a precipice. From the Square of St. Isaac's the travellers proceeded to their hotel on the English Quay, facing the Neva, and not far from the Nicholas Bridge. This is the fashionable afternoon promenade of St. Petersburg; and from their windows Mrs. Davenport and her daughter saw some of the highest nobility of the country, and among them the imperial family. Melicent was struck with the preponderance of military uniforms. "All of the gentlemen seem to be in the army," she remarked to her mother, "and yet Russia is not at war with any other nation. I wonder when these gayly-dressed fellows will be called on to lay down their lives for the Czar. Somewhere, very soon, I am sure. I am so impatient to begin my medical studies in order to be ready to follow the Red Cross on its next campaign, wherever it may be!"

Mrs. Davenport looked up wearily. "Don't begin immediately, dear," she said; "take a little time for sight-seeing first. I am sure we shall find St. Petersburg very interesting, and you will have no time to do it justice after you have once plunged into your studies."

NICHOLAS BRIDGE.

Melicent shrugged her shoulders impatiently. "I promise, mamma, to devote an hour every afternoon, perhaps longer, to driving with you; but I do want to begin my studies at once."

"Then, dear, the first step will be to obtain a private driver, whom we can depend upon, to take you regularly to the medical school, and to drive us about the city. We must not be left at the mercy of these *isvostchiks*, or drosky-men, though I think you managed very nicely this morning. What a very shocking language it is! I can't understand a word of it, but I am confident that it is much more profane than other languages."

Melicent laughed merrily. "I remember seeing somewhere," she said, "a story of a

THE COUNTESS MELINOFF.

foreigner who heard the Boots at his hotel repeating emphatically the word '*Tchetirnadtzat*,' and immediately jumped at the conclusion that such a disagreeable word must be an oath, and, accordingly, when angry with his driver, shouted at him in a very vigorous manner, '*Tchetirnadtzat, tchetir-r-r-r-nadtzat!*' but, as the word really meant only fourteen, the driver simply drove about from street to street, stopping inquiringly at the number fourteen."

The Davenports' first call was upon the Countess Melinoff, the sister of Captain Müller. She had already heard much of her brother's American friends, and received them most kindly. Count

MRS. DAVENPORT.

Feodor Melinoff, her husband, was an intelligent and courteous gentleman, whose duties kept him near the Czar. Their apartments were in a charming palace, and the ladies were immediately introduced into a delightful circle of Russian society. Melicent found that listening to the gay and witty conversation of the ladies who hovered in the after-

THE WINTER PALACE.

noon about the countess's samovar (tea-urn) was a very pleasant and effective way of studying the Russian language, and even Mrs. Davenport began to pick up and use the words which had seemed to her so unpronounceable.

They met many distinguished people, and Melicent was deservedly popular, as every true American girl is sure to be. One afternoon they witnessed a military review from the carriage of the countess, and, among the officers manœuvring the troops, the Grand Duke, several princes, and the two Generals Skobeleff, father and son, were pointed out, with General Gourko, and others, destined to become more famous in the approaching war. After the review, a young man rode up to the carriage, and was presented by the countess as Prince Tserteleff. He had visited England, and spoke English well. He impressed the ladies as a man of modesty and ability, and Mrs. Davenport asked if he were a soldier. "He is attached to the diplomatic service," replied Count Melinoff; "but he is a bright youngster: we shall hear of him again."

THE GRAND DUKE NICHOLAS.

A few days later Melicent had the honor of being presented to the Czar. She did not lose her self-possession, but told him, with simple dignity, how high a privilege she considered it to meet the man who had inaugurated his career by freeing fourteen million serfs.

"Do you know," he replied as simply, "who it is who is really responsible for that?"

"No, sire."

"It is our novelist Turgenef. I should never have thought of it but for him. I am fond of hunting, and, when his 'Memoirs of a Sportsman' was published, I said to myself, 'Here is something which will interest me.' And it did; but not in the way I had expected. The former serfs of Russia owe their liberation to that book."

DIMITRI DIMITRIE-VITCH.

Melicent could not consent to spend more than a very small portion of her time in society, but began her medical studies at once. Their coachman, Dimitri Dimitrievitch, whom they had obtained through their landlord, spoke English, and proved to be a jewel of intelligence; but, when so reported to the count, he exclaimed, "An intelligent coachman! Impossible! the only men of intelligence of that class are in the service of the detective police."

Count Melinoff had spoken at random, and Mrs. Davenport was far from taking alarm; but Dimitri Dimitrievitch was, in fact, a detective. The Davenports had been followed to their hotel by the little man who had dogged their steps from Vienna. He had explained to the landlord that it was necessary that his guests should be placed under police surveillance, and when Mrs. Davenport desired the landlord to secure a coachman, her request was sent to the police headquarters, and Dimitri, one of the best detectives on the force, was installed in his position.

Melicent's desire to study medicine strengthened the suspicions. Several of the medical students were *suspects*, and Dimitri watched carefully to see if Melicent cultivated the acquaintance of these persons. He was so obliging and competent that Mrs. Davenport employed him in many ways, and intrusted him more and more with her affairs. He

A MILITARY REVIEW.

knew all the acquaintances of both the ladies; he read every letter which they received or wrote; he did all their errands, and noted every circumstance, however slight. That the Count and Countess Melinoff should be their most intimate friends surprised him, for the count was an ardent supporter of the Czar, and a representative of the old aristocracy. When he took the ladies to the Countess Melinoff's first reception, and noted the liveries of the servants on the long line of carriages, and the crests upon the panels of the carriages, it seemed to him that his employers moved in a very respectable rank of society, and he reflected that, if they were "politicals," they must be very important and dangerous ones.

They were fond of visiting the different palaces, and remained, as it seemed to him, a long time in the picture-gallery of the Hermitage, and in the Imperial Library. Could it be that they were lying in wait to assassinate the Czar? It surely was not possible that they really cared anything for those smoky old pictures and musty books. Perhaps there was a plot to steal the crown jewels.

With all his vigilance, however, he could not discover anything implicating the ladies, until the latter part of the winter, when a mysterious letter arrived from Captain Müller, in which he referred to a plot which they had entered into with him, and inquired as to its success. The plot, of course, was Melicent's promise to induce Sallie to join her in St. Petersburg; but, as the Melinoffs were intending to remove for the early spring to their villa at Yalta, in the Crimea, Captain Müller suggested that they should all meet at the pretty residence of the countess, and begged Melicent to co-operate with him in urging Sallie and Alice to accept his sister's invitation. If the captain had only spoken of all this in plain language, Dimitri would have thought nothing of it; but the word *plot* revived his flagging suspicions.

It so chanced that a letter from Sallie fanned the flame: she spoke of the political situation in Bulgaria, and begged that Melicent would let her know whether there was any hope that the Czar would take up the matter, and declare war against the Turks. It chanced that Dimitri was cleaning the windows of Mrs. Davenport's boudoir when this letter arrived, and did not have his usual opportunity of a first perusal; but when Melicent locked it away in her desk, one leaf fluttered to the floor, and this he secured. The closing lines on the page ran as follows: —

"You know that I have always disapproved of bloodshed, but sometimes it seems the only check to tyranny, and so if the Czar"—

A SUSPICIOUS INTERVIEW.

Could anything be more conclusive? Melicent was certainly engaged in a plot to assassinate the Emperor.

He now watched Melicent more carefully than ever, and searched her trunks for dynamite bombs, and other infernal machines. One day, he saw her speaking to a woman in the park. The circumstance was natural enough, for the woman was a fellow-student; but Dimitri started with exultation: it was the first time that either of the ladies had held any communication with a "suspect." He strolled behind them in an agony of curiosity. If he could only hear one word of their conversation! and presently he did hear it. The woman's manner was excited: she gesticulated violently, but spoke in so low a tone that Dimitri, losing his caution, approached nearer, and heard her distinctly utter the name, "Natocha Melniketzky!" It was evident to Dimitri that this woman had recognized Melicent as the Nihilist that she had all along been suspected to be. This sudden discovery quite took away his senses, and deprived him of the power of immediate action, and, when Melicent turned and recognized him, as she immediately did, he could only stammer that the carriage was waiting for her at the corner. Melicent offered to take her friend home, but she declined the kindness, and stole swiftly away.

Dimitri drove his mistress home, cursing his own stupidity in not at once throwing off his disguise, and arresting both women. This stranger who had temporarily escaped him would be a most valuable witness against Melicent, and now he must wait until he could secure her.

So all winter Dimitri wove his web, like a malicious spider, and the unsuspecting Melicent fluttered cheerfully about within the toils.

CHAPTER XIII.

BALKAN ROSES.

THE winter was over, and spring, which comes early to the Turkish principalities, had covered the land with beauty.

The letter containing Captain Müller's declaration had been followed by many others. It had traversed the Atlantic to Sallie's parents, and had returned with the news that Mr. and Mrs. Benton would join their daughter in Russia in the summer. Sallie wished them to pass their judgment upon her friend before an engagement was entered upon; for to her an engagement was a very sacred thing, and not to be rushed into until after a season of probation and thorough acquaintance, wherein both parties might become very sure that their union was wise. Captain Müller — captain no longer, but, through her influence, simple Herr Müller — had consented to this, begging that she would visit during the coming summer with his sister, the Countess Melinoff. The countess had sent Sallie and Alice most sisterly invitations, which had been accepted, though the time of their going was continually put off by Alice, who could hardly be induced to take any vacation. Sallie, too, was growing more and more interested in her work. She could hardly believe the stories of cruelty and oppression which were told her, they seemed so at variance with the smiling aspect of all nature. She had wished to make a picture of a Bulgarian shepherd, guarding his flock in the fields, — the man was so picturesque in his black astrachan cap and his great-coat of sheepskin, with the wool turned inside, and the outer surface ornamented with an *appliqué* pattern in red cloth. The man had advised her not to paint in the fields. "The Turks come sometimes," he said. "I will pose for you in the courtyard of the school to-morrow."

"And you will bring some sheep, and hold one of the lambs in your arms, as you do now?" she asked. The attitude, as well as the costume, had struck her, it seemed so appropriate to the man's name, which was Kristo.

But the shepherd did not come in the morning, and Marika told her that his body had been found beside the well, where he had been watering his flock. The sign of the cross, cut deeply in the forehead of the murdered man by two sword-gashes, told that the crime had been committed by some one who hated him because he was a Christian. Kristo's sons suspected a Turkish neighbor, who had immediately seized upon the sheep; but, when they made complaint to the Cadi, the man asserted not only that the sheep were his own, but that he had seen the two boys commit the murder. They were, accordingly, thrown into prison. That they were not at once beheaded proved that the Cadi did not give entire credence to the testimony.

While the missionaries sympathized with the oppressed people, they realized that they held the little foothold which they had gained in the country through the sufferance of the Turkish Government, and that they were bound to take no part in politics. But Sallie felt that she was not so bound; and the more she saw of Turkish misrule, the more indignant she became.

Her first acquaintances, Katarinka and Marika, were still her favorites. The family had settled near the school, and the father was attempting to carry on his trade as a weaver of rugs. Every operation in their manufacture, from the raising of the goats for the hair, was performed by some member of the family. The youngest child watched the little flock, the girls spun the yarn, the mother, a second Lydia, prepared the dye-stuffs, and the father wove. The colors were very beautiful, and the recipes used in the dyeing were a secret, handed down in the family, perhaps from the very Lydia of Thyatira whose purple dye-stuff was so beautiful that Paul especially refers to it. Sallie had been struck by the rich colors when she first bought the yarn from the girls at Ragusa, and was still more delighted by the tasteful combinations shown in the finished rugs.

"You ought to make a good living," she said to the weaver; "for these prayer-rugs are very popular in Constantinople, and sell in the bazaars for a high price."

"I should get along very well," he explained, "if it were not for the taxes. Look at my goats. They are first taxed as live-stock; then their milk is taxed; their hair is taxed when it is clipped, and, again, if I sell it as yarn, the dye-stuffs are taxed, and the finished rugs must pay one-fifth to the Crown, one-fifth to the Pasha governing this pashalik, and another fifth as a special military tax. Then, last spring, I happened to make a very handsome rug, and the Pasha took a fancy to it, and bought it at his own valuation. Why did I not object? There was the bastinado. Everything that we buy is taxed — our food, clothing, the house we live in, every fruit-tree in the garden. It is a wonder how we live."

Sallie wondered, too. "Why do you remain in such a country?" she asked.

The weaver shrugged his shoulders patiently. "Where can we do better? And the school, the school makes up for much. I would suffer anything for my daughters. Trajan Evanova is a worthy man, and I hope soon to see Marika happily settled in life."

Easter was celebrated in Samokov with less rejoicing than is usual in the Greek Church. The steel bars, which take the place of bells, were beaten in the belfries, and the people greeted one another with the exclamation, "*Christus vuskrusny!*" ("Christ is risen!") and the reply, "*Vuskrusny nacesteena!*" ("He is risen indeed!") But their Turkish neighbors scowled in a way which boded no good, and the examination and exhibition of the mission-school were hastened by rumors of coming trouble. These exercises were very creditable to

A MARRIAGE PROCESSION IN BULGARIA.

the school, many Turkish officials of high rank attending, some out of curiosity possibly, but others from genuine interest. One pasha, of noble bearing, who had long shown himself friendly to the missionaries, advised them privately that the scholars should be sent to their homes, and that the teachers should leave the country at once. "It will not be a safe place for ladies much longer," was his warning. Two of the lady teachers took the train for Constantinople.

Trajan Evanova had insisted that the family of his betrothed should spend the summer with his parents at Batak, as this Balkan village was so far removed from the larger towns and ordinary routes of travel that it seemed to offer a safe harbor from any tidal wave of war which might sweep across the country.

Sallie and Alice were besought to visit with them, and to remain until after Marika's wedding, and decided to do so, as the wedding was to occur in a few days. Gus,

THE ROSE HARVEST.

after his tour with James Osborne, had settled at the boys' school at Philippopolis, where he was reading the "Odyssey" with a native Greek. His school had not closed, and Sallie thought it a good plan to fill in the interval, while awaiting him, by making this visit. They made the trip in the jolting wagons of the country; but the slopes of the Balkans were beautiful with wild-flowers, and much of the way they were climbing the mountain-paths in advance of their rude vehicles. The wild rose grew in abundance, and they were told that many of the mountain-girls earned their livelihood by collecting the roses, and distilling the precious attar, for which Turkey is so justly famed. The girls themselves were true roses, with soft, petal-like cheeks and deep, gentle eyes. As they fluttered by, Sallie distinctly perceived the scent of the roses. Batak itself was situated on a spur of the mountains, along a dashing stream, which turned the wheels of many saw-mills. A church, with a little graveyard, stood in the centre of the village, and a large schoolhouse was well filled with pupils. The houses were very simple. Trajan's parents had secured one for the family of the weaver. It was built of basket-work, plastered within and without with mud, and whitewashed. The roof was of curved red tiles, making a very picturesque appearance. The principal apartment served partly as kitchen and partly as stable, and the flickering firelight fell on the sporting children, while the cows munched their fodder in the shadowy corners. Sallie, tired as she was from her journey, took out her sketching material. "It is like the stable at Bethlehem," she said to Alice.

The room assigned to the young Americans was newly whitewashed and clean. Their couch was formed of rugs, spread on fragrant hay. They spent several days in this interesting village, and during their stay Marika's marriage was celebrated, Trajan urging that he was about to join the Bulgarian legion, and that he might be killed. "If so," he said, "I wish to leave Marika my goldsmith-shop and other property."

The wedding ceremonies were very curious. It was performed by the "pope," as the village priest was called, and, after the marriage in the church, there was a dance on the village green, to the music of a bagpipe. Trajan's presents were carried to his bride by a procession of friends. The wedding feast consisted of many courses, served on a long table, raised only six inches from the floor, on which the guests sat, for there were no chairs. The pottery was classical in shape, and brightly decorated, and the coffee was served from a brazen coffee-pot of beautiful shape.

It was with sincere regret that Sallie and Alice parted, a few days

INTERIOR OF BULGARIAN PEASANT DWELLING.

later, from their Bulgarian friends. The last picture which Sallie had of them showed the pretty bride standing in the doorway, with tears in her eyes, as she threw kisses toward them. Trajan left with the American girls, intending to conduct them to the nearest railway station, and then to rejoin his regiment. They found, however, that the trains had been stopped, and the rails torn up, for the Sultan had been using the road to send troops into the country. Trajan looked very grave: this measure could only delay for a short time the arrival of the Turkish forces. The outbreak had begun, and this action of the Bulgarians would furnish the Turks with an excuse for cruel reprisals.

They had continued their journey toward Philippopolis but a few miles, when they were met by fleeing peasants and townspeople.

PRINCESS NATHALIE.

"You are mad to go in that direction," one of them said. "The Turks are momentarily expected."

Trajan turned the horses. "We must drive to Samokov," he explained.

"But my brother!" Sallie exclaimed.

More questioning of the refugees elicited the fact that he had left

Philippopolis the day before with a gentleman whom Sallie surmised to be James Osborne. She decided at once that he had gone to Samokov to find her, and toward Samokov they immediately hastened. Pausing at Tatar Bazardjik to change horses, they were met at the inn-door by Gus and Mr. Humphrey. Gus reported that James Osborne, having accompanied him thus far, had placed him in Mr. Humphrey's care, and had himself gone to Batak in much anxiety as to the safety of the two girls, as he had heard that Achmet Azha was marching in that direction with his terrible Bashi-Bazouks. Trajan Evanova, on receiving this information, rushed away without bidding them farewell, lashing his jaded horse into a furious gallop.

PRINCE MILAN IV. OF SERVIA.

"You are only just in time to escape from the country by the north," said Mr. Humphrey. "Even now you may be cut off. You cannot leave by the west or northwest, for Servia and Montenegro have at last united in declaring war against Turkey, Prince Milan and Prince Nicholas having come to a definite agreement. No passenger steamers ply up and down the Danube at present, for the river is blockaded and fortified by both Servians and Turks. Nor can you leave the country by way of Constantinople, for the Turkish troops are on the march from that direction for Servia, and are committing frightful ravages on the way. They are desolating the country about Philippopolis. I hear of whole villages burned, their inhabitants indiscriminately massacred. Achmet Azha, with his Bashi-Bazouks, is dashing in every direction, pillaging and slaughtering in the district south and southeast of us. They may be at Samokov in a day or two. Your only possible way of escape is by the northeast. I will escort you to our friends at Eski Zagra. They will help you to cross the Balkans by the Shipka Pass. You will probably find the country north of the Balkans quiet, and your next step will be to cross the Danube at Rustchuk, and proceed to Bucharest, from which point you have rail communication with every part of Europe."

SERVIAN.

There was no time for hesitation; and Alice, Sallie, and Gus, led by the brave missionary, whose horseback tours as a colporteur had frequently taken him over this part of the country, were soon fleeing through the panic-stricken district to Eski Zagra, at the foot of Shipka Pass, the gate through the northern range of the Balkans. The wave of war had not actually reached this beautiful region, and the inhabitants were continuing their peaceful avocations.

SERVIAN.

They were hospitably entertained by the missionaries, and urged to rest for a few days, and obtain necessary passports, and make other preparations for their journey. Sallie wrote to her parents from this point, announcing her intention of meeting them at Moscow. It was hard, however, to induce Alice to continue the journey. "I am sure that I can be of use here," she said, "and I would much rather remain."

But on the third day James Osborne arrived. He had ridden hard, and, although nearly exhausted, was in a fever of impatience for them to leave the country with him.

"You do not know what I have seen," he repeated continually. "You must not wait for papers, or for anything else, but must come with me at once. I can get you through to Bucharest, I am confident, if we start at once; but every hour diminishes the chance."

On applying for a conveyance to take them across the mountains, they were informed that the Turks had fortified Shipka Pass, and had stopped all travel over the Balkans.

"Then we are really hemmed in on all sides!" Sallie exclaimed, in despair.

"Very well," Alice replied calmly, "I have been averse all along to running away. You know Jesus said, 'When ye shall hear of wars and rumors of wars, be ye not troubled,' but 'in your patience possess ye your souls.' We will stay right here, and accept whatever fortune comes to these poor people."

"By your leave," Sallie replied, "you do not know what you are talking about, and we will do nothing of the sort. In speaking of those very wars, Jesus told his followers to 'flee to the mountains.'"

"Yes," added Gus, "and to do it pretty lively, too — not even to stop to take anything out of the house, or to pick up his overcoat, if he was in the field. You don't catch me loafing around to do the martyr business, — that's certain."

Alice still demurred, but James Osborne said gravely, "This is no time or place for hesitation. I have left a country where thousands of men, women, and children are being butchered in cold blood, after having laid down their arms. I have seen sights too horrible to tell. You *must* come, if we have to carry you away by force."

"I wish we had remained at Batak," said Alice, with cheerful confidence, "for we can feel certain that, at least, Marika and Katarinka are quite safe."

James Osborne hesitated. "I do not know whether it is kind to undeceive you; but I reached Batak shortly after Achmet Azha left it. Isolated as the town is, it did not escape him, and he left it a charnel-house. The people gave up their arms, and were massacred, while unresisting children were burned alive in the schoolhouse, and over two hundred young girls were beheaded, their bodies piled in one great heap. I see no reason to hope that your friends were not among the number, for the town was completely surprised. I cannot tell you half the sickening story; but the entire population of that beautiful town was wiped out in one dreadful massacre, of which history hardly contains a parallel."

Alice turned deadly pale. "I will go," she said simply. "You are right; we can do nothing till this horror is overpast."

James Osborne prosecuted his inquiries in regard to the route with vigor. "There must be other passes across the mountains known to the peasants," he said.

Inquiry was made, and a young Bible-reader was found who had journeyed as a colporteur in the mountains. He knew of a disused pass not far from Kezanlik. It was hardly practicable for a wagon, he feared, but was a safe road for saddle-horses. The wagon was accordingly left behind, and the party proceeded on horseback, with a pack-mule for baggage. The girls had tried Turkish horses before, and found their gait an easy one. They take high steps, and bear their heads proudly, with a sort of processional march as though keeping time to music. Kezanlik — garden of roses — was embowered with flowers. Rumors of war had not reached it with any terrifying force, and all was quiet and peaceful. Their guide led them straight toward the mountain wall. "Surely there is no possibility of scaling that perpendicular cliff," said Sallie; but a little divergence to the right disclosed a gorge, with the nearly dry bed of a torrent, up which they mounted with perfect ease. Ferns grew beside them, trees sometimes arched over their heads, and in profusion on every hand grew the Balkan and Damascus roses. On each side the mountains rose, casting their cool shadows and making the ride a very pleasant one. A little past noon they gained the summit, and looked back for a farewell glance at Bulgaria. Kezanlik and Eski Zagra were in full view, their white walls glistening in the sun. Very peaceful and beautiful they looked. "It does not seem possible," said Alice, "that war can find them here."

"You do not know the Turks," James Osborne replied. "Batak was in as fair a region as this, and it has been left a horror of blood, fire, and smoke."

"How horrible!" shuddered Sallie. "Is there no remedy?"

"None but that of war. None unless the Russians march down and sweep the Turks out of the provinces and into Asia."

Sallie was silent. Were all her dreams of arbitration and peace on earth a mere phantasm,—a heavenly mirage for which the world was not ready? It seemed so, but it was very hard to give the theories up.

They had descended the northern slope of the Balkans, and received shelter for the night in a convent of nuns of the Greek Church, who are allowed far more privileges than their Roman Catholic sisters.

They were much interested in the dress of the two young American women, and especially in the different fashion of wearing the veil.

"Turkish women," they said, "cover their mouths carefully, and only expose their eyes. You, on the contrary, shroud your eyes in mystery, and leave your lips temptingly exposed. This would seem to them very immodest; but we know that a woman's safeguard is not in the way in which she wears her veil, but her own behavior."

From the convent they rode to the village of Gabrova, where the inhabitants eagerly inquired the news from the south.

Many of the young men had crossed into Servia, to join the army of Prince Milan.

"You are going north," the older men said. "Tell our story to the Czar; ask him to come and help us."

"I will tell it to the best of my ability," James Osborne promised, "and by God's help I will come again, and, when I come, the Russian army will be with me."

Through every town as they passed it was the same thing. "Tell Alexander."—"Ask Alexander to come and help us."

There were Turkish officials in every town

TWO WAYS OF WEARING VEILS.

and village, who might have stopped their progress, but for the friendliness of the peasants, who furnished them with fresh horses, with food and shelter, and with guidance. Mr. Osborne was arrested at Tirnova, but he was released on examination of his credentials, and they reached the Danube in safety. Here they were disappointed to find that all crossing had been prohibited, and that a Turkish gunboat lay at anchor to enforce this order.

"We might attempt it at night," Sallie suggested; but James Osborne shook his head. They were at the village inn, and suddenly an unusual bustle and tramping were heard in an adjoining room. A waitress popped into the apartment occupied by the young ladies, and announced that the Pasha in command of the gunboat had come on shore with some of his officers, and was dining at their inn.

"He is a European," she explained, "a renegade, who has embraced Mohammedanism, and has been rewarded with high office."

BUCHAREST.

"If he is a European," Sallie suggested, "he might be inclined to let us pass. I think we had better ask for an interview."

This daring proposition was accepted by the party. James Osborne's card was sent in, and the servant returned saying that the Pasha would receive not only the newspaper correspondent, but the entire party. They were ushered into the presence. Alice saw only a pale-faced man in Eastern dress, who kept his face slightly averted, and Mr.

Osborne, bowing respectfully, had begun his address, when Sallie suddenly exclaimed, "Mr. Norcross!"

It was indeed the secretary, who looked up with a strange expression of shamefacedness and triumph. Sallie recognized only the first, and disregarding his proffered hand, turned haughtily from him and left the room. Mr. Norcross flushed deeply. "I might revenge myself for this insult," he said to Mr. Osborne, "by refusing your request, but I will try to show you that I am not such a bad fellow after all. Here is a written order for a boatman to take you across the river. Show this handkerchief as a flag, and you will not be fired upon."

"I thank you for this favor," Mr. Osborne replied, "but I cannot help lamenting the step which you have taken."

Mr. Norcross waved his hand airily. "Your lamentations are quite gratuitous," he sneered. "Your sympathies appear to be on the other side. If you will take up arms we may have the pleasure of another sort of meeting."

"So be it," James Osborne replied gravely.

It was hard for Sallie to bring herself to accept the courtesy which Mr. Norcross had offered, but she was prevailed upon to do so by Alice, who argued that, as she had yielded to Sallie's urgent demand for flight, it was now her friend's turn to give up something.

Another day brought them to Bucharest, a city which, while it possesses mosques with domes and minarets, boasts also railway-stations, the telegraph, hotels, and European shops. As Gus remarked, they were at last safely in Europe; but they were not tempted to delay; and without pausing to rest from their journey, they hastily took the next train for Moscow.

CHAPTER XIV.

MOSCOW, NIJNI-NOVGOROD, AND THE CRIMEA.

IT was summer also in St. Petersburg, and Mrs. Davenport and her daughter were preparing to leave the city. Without knowing that Sallie and Alice were on their way to Moscow, they had also planned to spend a part of the summer in the ancient city. The Melinoffs had arranged to go with them; for Sallie had at last definitely set the time of her visit, promising to join the countess in the autumn, at her beautiful villa at Yalta, in the Crimea.

Fortunately for the Davenports, Dimitri Dimitrievitch brought his machinations to a crisis, at a time when their friends were able to defend them, or they might have been compelled to take a much longer journey, and have visited a far different portion of Russia than the smiling Crimea.

Count Feodor Melinoff happened to be in the bureau of the chief of the Gendarmes, when Dimitri brought in the letters from Captain Müller and Sallie, which were to be used as evidence that Melicent was a Nihilist. He listened carelessly to the detective's report. Two letters containing positive evidence against the suspect, Natocha Melniketzky. "Good!" said the officer. "The young woman was arrested this morning, and is now in prison, awaiting her examination. I am glad to have some additional testimony, for the evidence already received is not at all conclusive. You are relieved from duty on that case, and will receive another."

Dimitri passed into the next office for future orders. He was somewhat surprised to learn that Melicent was already arrested. Some other detective must have been upon her track, he thought. He

wondered if Mrs. Davenport were also in custody, but concluded that, all things considered, he would not return to the hotel to ascertain.

Meantime the count had been struck by something familiar in Dimitri's face; and as his eye fell on the letters lying before the officer, he suddenly recognized the handwriting of his brother-in-law, Captain Müller. "Who did you say has just been arrested?" he asked.

"Natocha Melniketzky, who has been masquerading under the assumed name of Melicent Davenport."

"Impossible!" exclaimed the count. "I know the young lady well."

"Here is the evidence. Can you disprove it?"

Count Melinoff read the letters hastily. "Fortunately, I can," he replied. "One is from my wife's brother, an ex-officer in the German army, whose entire career is well known. The 'plot' to which he refers is perfectly clear; in fact, it is explained farther on. It is simply a desire of his to have my wife invite his *fiancée* to visit us this summer. This other letter is from the young lady herself. You will see that she hopes the Russian Government will decide to make war upon Turkey. There is nothing revolutionary in that. Your 'evidence' amounts to nothing."

The officer listened carefully, and re-read the letters. "I believe you are right," he said. "Will you make this explanation in writing?"

"Certainly; and will make myself personally responsible for the good behavior of this young lady, whom we are about to take with us to the Crimea."

The officer promised that the matter should receive immediate attention, and the count returned to his home much excited. "My dear!" he exclaimed, as he stormed into his wife's boudoir, "have you heard the news? Our friend, Miss Davenport, has been arrested as a suspect."

"Impossible!" exclaimed the countess. "Calm yourself, my dear. You have been misinformed."

"But I tell you that I have just come from the Bureau of the Police, and that Melicent is now in prison, awaiting exile."

"Melicent has just been here," replied the countess. "She left the house but a moment ago. Look, there she is!"

The count stepped to the window, and saw the well-known figure of their friend, in a stylish costume, just turning the corner. She carried a natty umbrella, with which she tapped the pavement excitedly as she walked. "Miraculous!" exclaimed the count. "How did she effect her escape?"

"She has not even been arrested, but she came to see if anything could be done for a friend of hers, Natocha Melniketzky, a medical student, who has been thrown into prison on suspicion. I told her that it was very dangerous meddling with such matters; and you always made it a point to keep entirely aloof from them."

A WELL-KNOWN FIGURE.

The count sunk into an arm-chair with a groan. The countess flew to his assistance, and he finally recovered sufficiently to explain the situation. "And to think that I have become personally responsible for this unknown female!" he exclaimed, "who may be the worst of criminals."

The countess laughed merrily. "In that case console yourself. She will not be released."

"Oh, yes, she will! I brought all my influence to bear, and she will probably be discharged."

The countess grew pensive. "I think, Feodor, that all things will work together for good. If these letters were the only evidence against this poor woman, it was only just that they should be explained, and that she should be cleared."

"But what if the police insist on exchanging Natocha for Melicent, and in exiling our friend?"

"The administration would hardly do that; besides, we all leave St. Petersburg so soon, that the police will hardly have time to straighten the tangle before Melicent will be out of their reach."

"What a pity," said the count, "that your brother did not choose Miss Davenport, instead of this young lady who has such peculiar notions about war. I fear we shall not find her so charming as he paints her; and then, young ladies with ideas are very dangerous."

The administration, when it is a question of releasing a prisoner, works slowly, and Natocha seemed lost from their view. Everything had been done for her that was possible; and the Melinoffs and Davenports shortly afterward left the city in company. The Melinoffs were to be guests of the Davenports, for a time, at Moscow; the countess having been persuaded to this by a secret which Melicent had confided, and which had also been intrusted to Sallie and Alice, by James Osborne. The long engagement was to find its fruition at last in a happy marriage.

Mr. Ignatief, whom the newspaper correspondent had met in Montenegro, having decided to enlist in the Servian war, under Prince Milan, had offered the editorship of his paper in Moscow to James Osborne. It was the first time, in many years, that a quiet life had been possible for him. He was wearied with travel, but this alone would not have decided him. He saw in the position a possibility for his long delayed marriage with Melicent, and for beginning their home life. To Moscow, therefore, the little party of fugitives from Bulgaria had come. But as Sallie and Alice desired to surprise Melicent, James Osborne had not written that they were with him.

The girls had gone at once to the hotel, where Mr. and Mrs. Benton were waiting to meet their children, — not without much anxiety, for news of the trouble in Bulgaria had been telegraphed all over the world, and had reached them before Sallie's letter from Eski Zagra, which assured them of their safety.

Owing to the influence of the countess, the party from St. Petersburg took apartments in the Kremlin. Melicent found the city even more interesting than St. Petersburg. The view from a distance was very picturesque; the many towers, cupolas, onion-shaped domes and minarets, reminding one strongly of an Oriental city. The Kremlin, which is the aristocratic part of the city, stands upon a hill, separated from the lower town by a white wall, and looking, as it seemed to Melicent, like a tea-tray, crowded with a gold and silver service, flanked with a collection of pepper-pots and decanters with faceted glass stoppers. The countess had many friends residing in the Kremlin; and before the arrival of James Osborne, the ladies rode from palace to palace, admiring, most of all, the little casket-like Granovitaya Palata, which contains the coronation hall of the czars. Moscow, though no longer the capital, is still a royal city; and each emperor must receive his consecration here. The old city wakens to new life on the occasion of each coronation. The jewelled plate is brought forth from its vaults, tapestries are unfolded, and velvets dusted, gilding touched up; visitors flock to the city; and all the trades-people who thrive upon the extravagance of the rich, drive a flourishing business.

James Osborne arrived; and the countess, who had wished with all her heart that her brother were the bridegroom-elect, submitted him to very close scrutiny. A *fête* had been arranged in the gardens of the Petrovsky Palace, in the suburbs, which are thrown open to the public, and the party drove out together.

"You know this is the palace," the countess explained, "where outside the city the uncrowned emperor is made to wait three days, as though a suppliant for his rights, before he is brought to the Kremlin for his coronation."

"I ought to have been entertained here," Melicent said softly, "for I have come to the city to receive the crowning blessing of my life, — a trust more sacred than that of an empire."

THE GRANOVITAYA PALACE.

"Will my emperor graciously alight?" said James Osborne, with a smile; "your insignificant empire has prepared a little surprise, to grace your coronation."

As he spoke a lady left a little kiosk, where a party sat around a smoking samovar, and Melicent stood face to face with Sallie. It was a joyful meeting to all. The countess was drawn to her from the first, and a joyful afternoon was passed in the palace gardens. Very soon, however, the conversation took a serious turn, as Sallie and Alice told of the horror which they had left behind them; and again the question was asked, "What can be done to help these poor people?"

"Nothing," James Osborne replied, "but to drive the Turk into Asia."

"The Russian Government would like nothing better than to accomplish that result," said the countess; "but the Czar is only a figure-head after all. He can go only so far as popular sentiment will let him."

MELICENT IS SURPRISED.

"Popular sentiment is quite in that line," remarked the Count Feodor. "Russia desires an outlet to the south and a gate to Asia. The mouth of the Danube and Batoum are prizes which the popular consideration would think worthy of a war. It would be simple enough if we had only to consult our own people. Unfortunately, the opinion of the other great powers is to be considered, and, first, that of England."

"England shall place no obstacle in the way of this war," said James Osborne. "Popular sentiment controls the action of England, just as it does that of Russia. And the English people are Christians. They would far rather give up their own interests than pursue them at the cost of cruelty to a race. You shall see, the newspaper is the true monarch of the world. If it is popular opinion which shapes the action of governments, it is the newspaper which shapes popular opinion. I am here in Moscow as the editor of one of its leading journals. I shall fill my post poorly if, before the year is out, a strong war sentiment has not been created. J. A. MacGahan, one of the most talented and earnest of our war correspondents, is revolutionizing popular sentiment in England. Other writers are telling the truth in Austria, Germany, and France. Another year we shall be marching on Constantinople."

The countess was greatly interested; woman-like, she had already

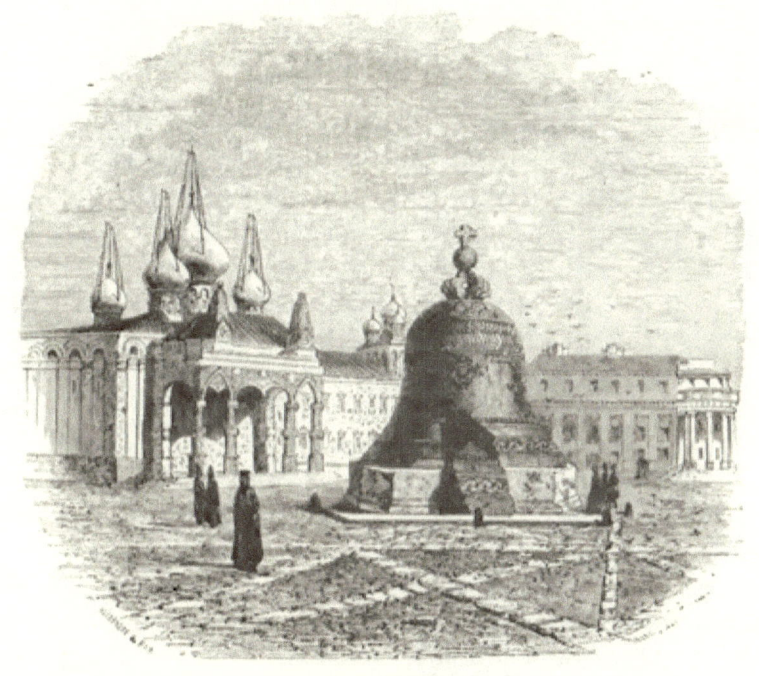

CZAR KOLOKOL.

busied herself in preparations for the simple little wedding, but she now entered into them with great enthusiasm.

While these arrangements were in progress, Gus amused himself by visiting all the places of interest in the city, and in guiding his father and mother, and others of the party, to them. He was especially interested in the history of the Vasili Blagennoy Church, built for Ivan the Terrible, in the grotesque, semi-barbaric Tartar style; and so delighting that monarch, that it is said he ordered the eyes of the architect to be put out, "in order that he might never build another like it."

"He must have been a sweet-tempered, fatherly old fellow," mused Gus. "Wonder if it wouldn't be a good thing for the world if some of our modern architects were rewarded in the same fashion. Certainly if they perpetrated any such glaring and frightful combinations of color in these days, some means would be found to keep them from repeating the crime against good taste."

Not only is the coloring of the church fearful and wonderful, but the eight domes are cut into the most fantastic forms imaginable, as Théophile Gautier has described them, "some beaten into facets, these cut into diamond points, like pine-apples, those in spirals; others, again, marked with scales, lozenge-shaped, or celled like a honey-comb."

The Tower of Ivan Veliki pleased him more. He frequently climbed to its top (325 feet) to obtain the grand view of the circling city. At its foot rests the famous Czar Kolokol bell (now broken), which was tolled at the birth of Peter the Great, but has been unused for two hundred years. It is said to weigh about two hundred tons; and "imagination's utmost stretch" quails before a contemplation of the thunderous tone which it must have pealed forth on the birth of the great emperor.

The bells were ringing in Moscow with a joyful clatter, welcoming the *fête* day of some saint, on Melicent's wedding morning. It was a simple wedding, with her dear friends only as witnesses; and, after it was over, they conducted her to her new home, and left her there. No reception or display of wedding presents, — though each friend gave his or her token of affection, — or bridal tour; for the life of both bride and bridegroom had been full of journeyings, and a quiet home seemed the greatest of luxuries.

After the wedding, Sallie applied herself to her painting. "I cannot stir the world with my pen, like James Osborne," she said, "but perhaps I can attract the attention of some to Bulgaria in another way.

CHURCH OF VASILI BLAGENNOY.

Surely, every form of expression, art as well as literature, has its moral obligation. I can tell people, with my brush, what I saw in Bulgaria."

She unrolled the canvases which she had brought from Samokov: Marika, with her pathetic look of heavenly sweetness and innocence; Katarinka, with fear and distrust stamped on her handsome features; and murdered Kristo, — with the lamb still in his arms, licking his sheltering hands, — and she painted with the inspiration of a new purpose. Herr Müller came to Moscow and watched her with surprise. "I did not know that you were a genius, Sallie. I am afraid that a woman with your talent has no right to be married, and to waste even a part of your life on me."

Sallie laughed lightly. "Don't be jealous of my art, Fritz. I shall lay it all aside by and by. It is only for this time, and for a particular purpose, that I am so absorbed in it. Be patient a little while, and I will give you all the attention you deserve very soon."

Friedrich Müller pulled his mustache meditatively. "I don't understand her," he said to himself. "I thought she loved me, and yet she turns me off as though I were of no account whatever."

Mr. Benton recognized the young man's chagrin, and applied himself to entertaining and becoming acquainted with his prospective son-in-law. Together they looked up the souvenirs of Napoleon's disastrous campaign, — Gus accompanying them, with great delight, to historic sites during the day, and reading aloud to them Tolstoï's novel, "Peace and War," and from histories in the evening. The dreadful story of how the great general, with an army of half a million of men, crossed the Niemen in June, 1812, the Russian generals retreating before him, and wasting the country as they went, so that the invader could with difficulty obtain supplies. Napoleon followed with resolution, though a hundred thousand of his followers dropped off. He reached Smolensk in August, only to find it fired by the inhabitants. On the 7th of September he overtook the Russians and fought the battle of Borodino. Desperately he persevered, and reached Moscow a week later. And again, as in Smolensk, he found that so invincible was the pluck of the Russians, that they had destroyed their property rather than allow it to fall into the hands of the French. He rested in the city for five weeks, endeavoring to refit his army, which was now reduced to a hundred and twenty thousand men. Shortly after his arrival, a destructive fire broke out, — set by criminals, who had been released for that purpose. Nothing was left for him to do but to return; and now winter had set in. His veterans dropped in the snow, dying daily upon the marches. The Russians hovered in the rear, harassing his retreat. When he crossed the Beresina, on the 27th of November, his magnificent army had dwindled to twenty-five thousand. His pride and his power were broken. It was a death-blow to both.

The poet Southey has described the campaign, in one of his minor poems, — a satire not so familiar to us as to our fathers. Mr. Benton repeated it one evening. He had learned it as a boy, he said, to recite in school, merely as a feat of memory, because the names seemed to him so unpronounceable and absurd. Many of these names were familiar to the party, as belonging to nobles and generals already distinguished, and others were destined soon to come to the front.

THE MARCH TO MOSCOW.
BY ROBERT SOUTHEY.

The Emperor Nap he would set out
On a summer excursion to Moscow.
The fields were green and the sky was blue.
    Morbleu! Parbleu!
What a pleasant excursion to Moscow!

Four hundred thousand men and more
Must go with him to Moscow.
There were marshals by the dozen,
And dukes by the score,
Princes a few and kings one or two.
While the fields were so green and the skies so blue.
Nothing would do but the whole crew
Must be marching away to Moscow.

But the Russians stoutly they turned to,
Upon the road to Moscow.
Napoleon had to fight his way all through :
They could fight, though they could not parlez-vous.
But the fields were green and the sky was blue,
And so he got to Moscow.

He found the place too warm for him,
For they set fire to Moscow.
To get there had cost him much ado,
And then no better course he knew,
While the fields were green and the sky was blue,
But to march back again from Moscow.

The Russians they stuck close to him
All on the road from Moscow.
There was Tomazow and Jemalow,
And all the others that end in ow;
Milardovitch and Jaladovitch,
And Karatschkowitch,
And all the others that end in itch.
Schamscheff and Sochosaneff
And Schepaleff,
And all the others that end in eff.

And Platoff he played them off,
And Shouvaloff he shovelled them off,
And Krosnoff he crossed them off,
And Tuchkoff he touched them off,
And Boroskoff he bored them off,
And Kutousoff he cut them off,
And Parenzoff he pared them off,
And Woronzoff he worried them off,
And Doctoroff he doctored them off,
And Rodinoff he flogged them off.
They stuck close to Nap with all their might :
They were on the left and on the right,
Behind and before, by day and by night,
And then came on the frost and snow
All on the road from Moscow.

> The wind and the weather, he found in that hour,
> Cared nothing for him nor for all his power, —
> For him who while Europe crouched under his rod
> Put his trust in his fortune and not in his God.
> Worse and worse every day the elements grew;
> The fields were white and the sky was blue.
>   Sacrébleu! Ventre-bleu!
> What a horrible journey from Moscow!

During the reading of "Peace and War," the little circle had become greatly interested in the author. "How much I should like to meet him!" Sallie chanced to remark.

"That can be easily arranged," replied Count Melinoff. "Count Leo Tolstoï was a comrade of mine in the army. I have seen little of him since he adopted a literary career, though we were all very proud of his honors, and sorry to learn that he had renounced them all for the sake of living among the peasants as a peasant, and earning his bread by cobbling. His theories would have impoverished him but for his excellent wife, who possesses a fortune in her own right, which, fortunately, he has not the power to give away. He lives upon her estate at Krasnoe, not far from Tasnaya Polyana. If you like, we will make an excursion and visit them."

This visit was among the most pleasant of Sallie's Russian souvenirs. A son of the family awaited them at the station, with a carriage, and the Countess Tolstoï received them on the steps of her country-house. The count, they were told, was ploughing the field of a poor widow, who lived near by. The countess was evidently very proud of her generous but eccentric husband, and listened with pleasure to the praise which her guests rendered of his "Peace and War." She showed them his study, with its tool-bench and plain writing-desk. The count arrived in time for dinner, and changed his peasant's smock for a plain coat. The dinner was an excellent one, — of several courses, — but the count was extremely frugal, denying himself wine, and even tea. He told them the story of the poor widow whom he had been assisting. "Her husband died last winter, and, assisted by her little daughter, she buried him, — carrying the cross, which was to mark his grave, to the cemetery, — not having money to pay the sexton, or any friends to bid to the funeral. That woman has worked all her life for a pittance," he said. "What right have I to more? It is the same as if I had inherited a plantation of slaves in your own country. What would a Christian do there but renounce them all? So I renounce wealth obtained from the toil of others, and will possess nothing which I have not earned, which any one may not earn. It is my understanding of Christianity."

Sallie was much impressed by her interview with this singular man; and, on her return to Moscow, painted a sketch of the scene which he had described. The countess looked at it very kindly. "Our poor women in Russia all *bear the cross*," she said simply.

The count and countess went early to their villa in the Crimea, urging the Bentons and Alice to accompany them; but, as the weather was still warm in the south, and Mr. Benton wished to attend the fair of Nijni-Novgorod in September, the visit was deferred.

During their stay at Moscow, Sallie received a letter from Lady Saunters, who remembered her talent for painting, and wished to secure something of hers as a present for her husband. To Lady Saunters, therefore, Sallie sent the picture of Marika, telling her of the girl's tragic fate, and asking if she remembered meeting her at Ragusa. At the same time she made inquiries as to the means for having her painting of Kristo exhibited in London. In due time, partly through Lady Saunters, but also on account of its own merit, the painting was hung at one of the great exhibitions, where it attracted much attention, and helped usher in the strong and popular feeling of indignation which followed the report of the Bulgarian massacres.

Lady Saunters was so strongly moved by it that later she went out to Servia, with a party of friends, to assist in establishing an asylum for orphans. Alice, who had been watching eagerly for an opportunity to return to the provinces, immediately joined her; and only her parents' urgent remonstrances, and her own feeling that she was perhaps doing as valuable work for the cause by her painting, detained Sallie. The Servian war had ended ingloriously, only serving to bring much suffering upon the unhappy Bulgarians, and as yet none of the foreign powers seemed inclined to come to the help of the oppressed principalities; and an even deeper cloud of despair seemed to be settling upon them.

In September, the Bentons, Alice Newton, and Friedrich Müller visited Nijni-Novgorod.

The great annual fair has lost much of its prestige. Merchants no longer come from foreign lands in such numbers as formerly to attend it, but it is still an event of great interest to the city, and to the stranger who desires to become acquainted, at the expense of little travel, with the different types of Russians; for representatives from every part of Russia come to Nijni-Novgorod at the time of the fair. The town is admirably situated for such a trysting-place. It is not its only advantage that it is on the Volga, — the great water thoroughfare of Russia, — a vast river which has aptly been described as the spinal cord of the nation, carrying the currents of life through the immense body, and a highway to the Caspian and to Asia. The Oka joins the Volga at Nijni, bringing trade from Moscow and the west; and by an intricate system of canals, water communication is obtained with the Baltic, through Neva and St. Petersburg, with the White Sea on the north and the Euxine on the south.

Gus was surprised to learn that fifteen thousand vessels ply on the Volga alone. A forest of masts framed the city; and busy tugs were towing in the loaded barges with merchandise for the fair. They strolled, the first night after their arrival, among the booths, and interested themselves in the various types and nationalities of the merchants, as well as in the goods which they offered for sale. Here were the long-haired, mild-faced men of Moscow, with weapons as noted in earlier times as those of Damascus; and close beside them were pearl-inlaid and jewelled-handled daggers from the Turkish dominions. Here were rugs of Daghestan, and silks of Bokhara; furs from Siberia, — the softest and lightest sables, with creamy ermines, and silver and black fox. There were wonderful gems in the jewellers' bazaars, from the mines of the Urals. Alexandrite, with its wonderful emerald and ruby lights, and caskets, vases, and tables cut from streaky malachite, with gold and silver ware enamelled in colors. Not far from these choice objects were the fish-booths, where pretty girls from Pskov, with wonderful structures upon their heads, sold caviare and other salted fish; while peasants from villages, devoted to the manufacture of one particular article, brought axes or linen goods or leather, as the case might be. There was a band of Kirghiz in the outskirts, with beautiful horses for sale, who were carrying on a sort of impromptu circus; and a rival band of Calmuck Tartars from Kazan. Pilgrims from the Holy Land offered olive-wood rosaries to the devout; while

CALMUCK TARTAR MAID.

a nondescript in an Astrakhan cap, who had worn a scarlet fez at the opening of the fair, but had found it unpopular, peddled perfumes and soaps, and other wares suggestive of Constantinople. Mrs. Benton bought some of the famous brick-tea, brought by caravan overland from China, and said to be far superior in flavor to that transported by sea.

On the last evening of their stay at Nijni, they all mounted the Tower of Minin, and enjoyed the sparkling panorama of the lighted booths.

"How well Edna Dean Proctor describes it," said Sallie. "Her Russian poems have all of them a reality which spreads the entire scene before you, and the ring of life in their cadences, but none more so than

"'THE FAIR AT NIJNI NOVGOROD.'

"'Now, by the Tower of Babel,
   Was ever such a crowd?
Here Turks and Jews and Gypsies,
   There Persians haughty-browed;
With silken-robed Celestials,
   And Frenchmen from the Seine,
And Khivans and Bokhariotes,
   Heirs of the Oxus plain.

Here stalk Siberian hunters,
   There tents a Kirghiz clan
By mournful-eyed Armenians
   From wave-girt Astrakhan;
And Russ and Pole and Tartar,
   And mounted Cossack proud,—
Now, by the Tower of Babel,
   Was ever such a crowd?'"

One day the travellers saw a gang of convicts passing on their way to Siberia, and Sallie was reminded of the story which Melicent had told her of Natocha, and scanned the sad, hopeless faces, wondering if she were of the number.

Friedrich Müller was impatient to conduct the party to his sister's home at Yalta, and early in October the Bentons, accompanied still by Alice, turned their faces southward.

The Crimea has rightly been called the Italy of Russia. Here an entirely different climate is met, and the olive, the plum, the peach, and the date make the peninsula a second Greece. The countess's villa was situated half-way between the watering-place of Yalta and the royal pleasure resort of Livadia. It hung like a gull's nest to the high cliff, whose base was washed by the blue waters of the Euxine, and from the sea the white walls of the villa were hardly to be distinguished from those of the cliff itself. A staircase cut in the rock led down to the lapping water, and was almost sprinkled with the spray of a cascade which leaped over the same cliff. On the landward side, groves, vineyards, and gardens separated the villa from the public drive. It was a lovely spot in which to dream and bask in the sun or rest in the shadow and forget the world. But Sallie could not quite forget that there were human beings very near, leading far different lives; and though Friedrich was always pleading for a ride, or the countess planning an excursion by yacht to Balaklava and Sebastopol, or a carriage drive to a grand *fête* at the Emperor's palace at Livadia, Sallie still managed to secure studio hours, and to paint. Mr. Benton and Gus made the trip to Sebastopol, and found many interesting traces of the great siege of 1854 and 1855. Tolstoï has given a most realistic description of the fighting here, from the Russian side. The enemy, French and English, had taken positions on the landward side of the fortress. The Russians were shut up in earthworks and bomb-proofs, and endured patiently an iron rain of shot and shell, in the hope of a rescue which did not come; for the land forces were beaten at Balaklava and at Inkerman. All through the terrible winter and more terrible summer, the plucky besieged held out until September, when the Malakof redoubt was taken by the French, and the siege was at an end. Mr. Geddie states, in his "Russian Empire," that in one single day seventy thousand projectiles were thrown into Sebastopol, and the thunder of the cannonade was heard for sixty miles around. "One of the most singular illustrations of the enormous waste of material during the siege is the fact mentioned by Sir E. J. Reed, that the Russian Government, by imposing a tax of sixpence per hundredweight on the old metal picked up by the townspeople after the bombardment, were able to realize the sum of fifteen thousand pounds."

But the waste of precious life was still more reckless. In the last twenty-eight days of the siege Rambaud states that the Russians lost eighteen thousand men. Friedrich Müller was talking over these statistics with Sallie, the day after his excursion to Sebastopol.

"When I think soberly of such a siege as this," he said, "of Napoleon's Russian campaign, and of my own experiences with the German army, my reason admits that you are right. War is frightful barbarism. But when I turn from these considerations, and look at the pictures you are painting, and hear your stories of the barbarities of the Turks, I am all on fire. And if the Russians were on the march for Bulgaria, I am just as sure that every instinct of a man within me would cry to me to enlist in their service. I don't understand, Sallie, what your object is in painting such pictures as that, when you declare that you are opposed to war."

"But is there no other means of righting these wrongs, — arbitration, Christianity?"

Friedrich made a gesture of disgust. "Visionary remedies, for which the world is not ready. I tell you, Sallie, that you must stop concerning yourself about your fellow-men at all, or else be willing to die for them."

"I am willing to die for them," Sallie replied simply, "but do not see our right to murder other fellow-beings for them. If I only knew what ought to be done!"

"Since the problem is too difficult for you, why not wash your hands of the entire matter, and let us live for ourselves and for each other."

"That is not worthy of you, Friedrich."

"I know it; but the world is very beautiful,—just here,—and you are beautiful, too, Sallie, and I love you, and have given up the life of a soldier for you,—and with it all responsibility for righting the wrongs of the rest of the world."

"And I would be very unreasonable not to be satisfied. I will paint no more, Friedrich; you have showed me that I am only rousing people to indignation, without showing them a better way."

But the mischief was done. Friedrich Müller, slow to perceive, slow to move, was moved at last. The winter slipped away in the lovely Crimea; and one day in the early spring of 1877 the family were attending a *fête* at the royal palace at Livadia, which was built by Count Potocki, in the style of the palace of the old Khans of Crim Tartary at Baktchi-Serai. Sallie was chatting gayly with a member of Prince Vorontzof's family, who had driven over from the prince's Moorish palace at Alupka,—an ancient diplomat, full of reminiscences of the Potemkins, the Galitzins, and others.

THE OLD DIPLOMAT.

"Ah!" said he, "no opportunities are afforded to our young men to gain distinction nowadays. The manly art of war seems to be forgotten. I was discussing a very able article in the Moscow —— [naming James Osborne's paper] with his Imperial Majesty lately. It clamored for war, and his Majesty seemed to feel the justice of the arguments advanced; but an emperor is not moved by his own inclination, or his own sense of justice even, much less by anything written by a literary man, but by considerations of state policy alone."

"His Majesty was graciously pleased to admit to me," said Melicent, "that he had once been influenced to a great reform by something written by a literary man. Who knows but it may happen again?"

The diplomat twirled his lorgnette in airy incredulity.

Just then an officer entered the salon: there was a sudden hush, and then a buzz as of swarming bees. "What is it?" asked the old gentleman. "Only, sir," replied Count Feodor, "that the young men of Russia have now an opportunity of earning decorations for heroism. The Czar has declared war with the Porte!"

Exciting days followed. There had been much discussion as to Friedrich Müller's future manner of life, and it had finally been decided that he should emigrate to America and begin a mercantile life. But from that evening at Livadia his entire bearing changed; and one day he came to Sallie, as she sat in the garden, looking away toward the shores of Bulgaria, and, taking her hands, said gravely, "I gave up the army for your sake, and I will hold to that renunciation if you still demand it. But it is you who have rekindled the war spirit within me; and my brother-in-law has just obtained for me an appointment to General Gourko's staff. Shall I accept it?"

Sallie turned deadly pale. "It is the only way. You are right. There is no hope of any other deliverance for those people. It is a war of principle, and I will not keep you back."

CHAPTER XV.

SHIPKA PASS.

*From the smoking hell of battle,
Love and pity send their prayer,
And still thy white-winged angels
Hover dimly in our air.*

WHITTIER.

HOW events seemed to gather themselves into a whirlpool and twirl on to one great vortex after this!

The beautiful life at the villa was at once broken up, and the friends scattered. Count Melinoff and Friedrich, once more Captain Müller, joined the Russian army at Bucharest.

Sallie's parting gift to her lover was the pair of epaulets which he had sent her when he gave up his career for her sake. They needed to be only slightly changed to be adapted to his new uniform; and Sallie had embroidered them with fresh gold thread, tarnishing their brightness slightly with tears, which were shed in secret.

James and Melicent Osborne wrote that they had started in the same direction, — James Osborne as war correspondent, and Melicent having taken service with the Red Cross. "I must go too," Sallie had said. "I cannot bear to be left behind, and to do nothing."

THE EPAULETS RETURNED.

"Then," said her father, "I shall go with you. I was a hospital steward during our own war, and I don't believe I have forgotten my profession. We will join your friends at Bucharest, and offer our services to the Red Cross."

Gus was wild to join the expedition, but his father forbade it. "Your studies have been interrupted long enough," he said. "You must escort your mother back to America, and enter college this fall."

Since Florence Nightingale's administration at the hospital of Scutari, woman's place by the side of wounded and dying men has been undisputed. Sallie had read the account of the Crimean war with great interest. The wounded English soldiers were carried back from Sebastopol to Scutari, and here their condition, before the coming of the English nurses, is described by an eye-witness, Dr. Hamlin, as horrible. "Five thousand patients, in all forms of disease and suffering, with not half the force necessary to care for them. The smell of the hospital was nauseous, and the sights and sounds were such as untrained nerves could not endure. Cursing and praying, the maniac's shout or song, and the groans of pain or death, were mingled as they never were before. A noble-looking soldier said: 'At ten o'clock the lights are put out, and no one comes near us till morning. Some are crying, "Water, water!" some are praying; many are insane; some are dying. Those who ought not to move try to do something in the dark for the suffering. Oh, sir! our nights are terrible.'"

In this state of the hospital, Mr. Hamlin was informed, "Fancy! *some women* have come to take care of this hospital! Was ever anything more improper? I can assure you they won't stay long!"

But the women staid. A great reform was inaugurated. "Dividing the work among them, there was a nurse to each long corridor, walking back and forth all night, administering to the wants of sufferers, kneeling at the bedside of the dying," and imparting cheer to the convalescent. All the world has sung the praises of the woman who led this enterprise — none more worthily than Sidney Dobell. And this poem of his to Florence Nightingale was written on a page of Sallie's journal, with pressed flowers from Sebastopol.

> "How must the soldier's tearful heart expand,
> Who from a long and obscure dream of pain,
> His foeman's frown imprinted on his brain,
> Wakes to thy healing face and dewy hand!
> When this great noise has rolled from off the land,
> When all those fallen Englishmen of ours
> Have bloomed and faded in Crimean flowers,
> Thy perfect charity unsoiled shall stand!"

Sallie knew that the real horrors of war are seen in the hospital, not on the field of battle, and her repugnance for such scenes was intense. This was the same country in which Florence Nightingale had labored : the same terrific climate; the same Russian camps, with their lack of sanitation, on one side, and the only difference lying in the fact that the Turks took the place of the English, replacing civilized war by savage barbarities.

She knew that Russian hospitals were worse than English ones,— for she had read Tolstoï's account of the Russian side of that terrible Crimean campaign, and her courage quailed before the great novelist's description of

"A RUSSIAN HOSPITAL.

"You have scarcely opened the door before the sickening odor emitted from forty or fifty amputations or severe wounds makes you gasp for breath. You will behold frightful scenes here. You are seeing war, now, without the brilliant accompaniment of handsomely uniformed troops and inspiring music, of standards floating gayly in the breeze. You are seeing it as it really is, — in its blood, its suffering and death! The stretcher-bearers were continually bringing in new victims and laying them, side by side, in rows on the floor. The pools of blood, the feverish breath of several hundred men, created a heavy, fetid atmosphere, in which the candles burned but dimly; while a confused murmur of moans, sighs, and death-rattles, broken by piercing shrieks, filled the hall."

But even here an alleviating touch is given to the picture, for the author continues, —

RUSSIAN MILITARY TYPES.

"Sisters of charity, whose calm faces expressed an active, helpful interest, glided quietly about, carrying medicines, water, bandages, and lint."

It was some little time before the Red Cross brigade were called to render active service, and Sallie interested herself in watching the different types of men mustering to Bucharest, to the command of the Grand Duke Nicholas. The Circassian Cossacks, in their red and

COSSACKS ON THE ROAD FROM GALATZ.

green silk blouses, were certainly the most picturesque, but the Cossacks of the Don were more interesting. They were little men, with long, straight hair, and shrewd, merry faces,—described by an eye-witness as being all great-coat and boots, and more armed than any men of their inches in Europe. Their most characteristic weapon was the long, black lance; but they carry also a carbine, a revolver, and a curved sword. They rode wiry little ponies, "of indomitable toughness and gameness; fresh when most other horses are knocked up. They ride about alone with despatches, and escort suspected spies, keeping the head of their lance within easy distance of the small of the suspect's back, to be handy for skewering him if he attempted escape."

Sallie noticed that some of them wore a bit of dried weed twisted about their shakos; and she remembered the superstition described by Tolstoï, of the bursting weed, devoutly believed in by the Cossacks of the Don.

It is their custom to imprison a turtle over night, within a small palisade of sticks. In the morning it will be found that the captive has escaped; and at the point where he broke through his prison will be seen a bit of tangled weed. Take this and preserve it carefully, for as long as you wear it no bolts or bars will be able to keep you a prisoner.

After the Cossacks came the infantry in great divisions, making long marches across the muddy country, keeping time with long, swinging strides to their singing,—songs which she could not understand, but which she felt must mean,—

> "Hail to the day when the Eagles
> And the Cross shall gain their own."

They had sweet, strong voices, and they sang as if they were inspired, forgetting all weariness, and tramping on erect and fresh, when the cavalrymen swayed asleep in their saddles.

Among the Red Cross nurses, Melicent found an old friend,

Natocha Melniketzky, the suspected Nihilist. "Tell Count Melinoff," she said to Melicent, "that he need feel no uneasiness as to my behavior. It was very noble in him to be my security, and I shall not abuse his kindness. I have taken the oath of allegiance to the Czar, and I shall keep it. Now that I have experienced the kindness of one man belonging to the nobility, I feel differently toward the whole order."

Melicent did not explain that it was all a mistake.

In this period of suspense and preparation, the Red Cross had one patient in their hospital tent, whose coming to them happened in this wise. At Galatz, a Turkish turret ship was noticed on the Danube, followed by two gunboats; and four tiny Russian torpedo boats were sent out to blow it up. These torpedo boats were small steam launches, covered with sheet iron and painted black. They puffed gently along in the dead of night, the noise they made almost drowned by the croaking of the great frogs, and undiscovered until two of them were just under the great ironclad, when they were challenged; and they heard men running about on deck. The officers on board the little launches fastened their torpedoes under the hull of the ship, and darted their boats back the length of the electric wire, which connected the torpedoes with the battery. The officers established the connection of the electric current, and two terrible explosions were heard; a huge volume of water, carrying parts of the shattered ship, rose into the air, and a moment later the monitor was seen to be sinking; and presently only her masts, still flying the Crescent flag, were seen above the water. Two men were rescued from the doomed crew by the Russians, — one died immediately, the other was carried in a mangled condition to the hospital. He reported that the name of the gunboat was the "Lutfi Djelil," and that she carried two hundred men. Sallie did what she could for the poor man. One day it occurred to her to ask him if he knew of Mr. Norcross. The man appeared to understand her broken Turkish. Yes, he knew of the

RUSSIAN OFFICERS TAKING THE TURKISH FLAG.

English Pasha. He was high, high up in the favor of the Sultan, and very, very skilful. No torpedo boats would catch him.

Mr. Osborne was not sure that the man referred to their old acquaintance, but thought that he might mean Hobart Pasha, the admiral of the Turkish fleet, also an Englishman. Hobart Pasha, who has since published his recollections of the Russo-Turkish War, and has assured us that if his advice had been taken the Russians would not have crossed the Danube as easily as they did. As it was, the Turkish fleet caused them much annoyance.

Sallie wondered if they should hear more definitely from Mr. Norcross, and a little later they were destined to do so. The Russian torpedo boats did effective work in clearing the Danube, and making the crossing of the Russian troops a possibility. One Turkish monitor, however, gave them a gallant fight. It was attacked by four torpedo launches, but with a far different result from that of the affair of the "Lutfi Djelil." James Osborne had obtained permission to go out with the attacking party,— but the newspaper report of this action will be the briefest and the most authentic which we can give.

"This monitor, it soon became evident, was handled and commanded in a very different manner from the others with which the Russians had to deal. With wonderful quickness and skill she was prepared for action. Her commander began by likewise thrusting out torpedoes on the end of long spars, thus threatening the boats with the danger of being blown into the air first, at the same time opening a terrible fire with small arms and mitrailleuse. He besides tried to run the boats down, and very nearly succeeded. The reason soon became evident. The commander was a European, and, as the Russians believe, an Englishman, who directed the movements from the deck. He was plainly visible all the time, and was a tall man, with a long, blond beard, parted in the middle. He stood with his hands in his pockets, giving orders in the calmest manner possible.

"The torpedo boats continued their attempts for more than an hour. The monitor, active in trying to run them down, backing and advancing, turning and ploughing the water into foam as she pursued or avoided her tiny but dangerous adversaries,— a lion attacked by rats. One Russian officer, seeing the captain of the monitor coolly standing on deck with his hands in his pockets, emptied his revolver at him,— three shots, at a distance of not more than forty feet. The captain of the monitor, in answer, took off his hat and bowed, not having received a scratch. Later, however, the gallant fellow seems to have been killed or wounded, for he suddenly disappeared from the deck. The monitor immediately afterward retired precipitately from the scene of action."

Sallie was sure that she recognized Mr. Norcross in the chief actor in this affair. The only discrepancy was the beard; and there had been time for him to cultivate one. "They that take the sword shall perish by the sword," she thought, and then grew startled as she realized that this applied also to the Russians, and that Captain Müller might be the next brought in to the hospital.

The crossing of the Danube was accomplished by the main body of the Russians, during the last days of June, at Simnitza,— not without hot fighting, however; for the Turks realized that the Danube was their first barrier, and defended it bravely if ineffectually.

Prince Tcherkasky, the head of the Red Cross organization, had now enough to do. Prince Tolstoï directed the hospitals at Simnitza, where fully four hundred wounded were being cared for in an orderly and admirable manner; for as yet the tents were not overcrowded, or the nurses overworked. The weather, however, was now intensely hot. At Fratesti, on the Bucharest Railroad, two hospital trains,— one from Dresden, and one from Moscow, under the charge of the Countess Orloff and a staff of trained lady nurses,— waited to convey the wounded out of the country; while a committee of relief, in which the Countess Melinoff labored, was busily at work at St. Petersburg.

THE RED CROSS AT WORK.

The Emperor visited the hospitals and distributed thirty crosses of St. George, to the most valiant of the wounded.

The next barrier to be crossed was the Balkans. Everywhere between the Danube and the mountains, the Russian army was received by the Bulgarians with acclamations of extravagant joy. Church-bells which had not been rung for centuries pealed forth their welcome clamorously. Processions of girls in white, singing songs, and of children, bearing garlands of flowers, headed by the clergy with banners and censers,— and in one instance with an illuminated Bible, which had been hidden for years in a monastery,— streamed out to meet the army.

James Osborne, as he rode beside General Skobeleff, said triumphantly, as the chief men kissed his hands, "Did I not tell you that I would come again with the Russians?"

But the Turks, though they had retreated from Rustchuk with their commander-in-chief, Abdul Kerim, were not beaten. They were watching their opportunity, which they believed would come when the Russians attempted to storm Shipka Pass. Osman Pasha, too, was hastening from the west to Plevna, ready to fall upon the rear of the Russians, should they advance too recklessly; while Suleiman Pasha, who had been victorious in Montenegro, had just been transported by the Turkish fleet, with his army of forty thousand men, from the coast of Albania to Salonica (a distance of eight hundred miles, in twelve days), and was now waiting, ready for action, at Adrianople. (See map on interior of covers.)

The Russians, after crossing the Danube, separated into three divisions: that on the right, commanded by General Krudener, swept the country toward the southwest, while that on the extreme left, under the Czarewitch, performed the same office toward the southeast. The central column, commanded by General Gourko, was to attempt the crossing. He knew that Shipka Pass was strongly fortified by the Turks, and he deputed Prince Tserteleff to discover some other pass which would be practicable for artillery. It chanced that the Prince, who had met Melicent at St. Petersburg, discovered her among the Red Cross nurses on the very day that he was intrusted with this perilous duty. He informed her of his commission, and she immedi-

RECEPTION OF THE CZAR BY THE CLERGY.

ately told him of the Hainkoi Pass, through which Sallie and James Osborne had come on their flight from Bulgaria. The Prince listened attentively, and, disguised as a Bulgarian peasant, he went in search of it. The Bulgarians were everywhere helpful, and, to his delight, he found it unfortified. And, though the roadway had been broken in upon by mountain torrents, with a very little engineering he saw that it could be made passable for the light field-cannon, and even for baggage-trains. He accordingly returned and reported his success to General Gourko, who, leaving a division to advance on Shipka Pass from the north, under Prince Mirsky, hastened across the mountains by the Hainkoi Pass, to the attack of Shipka from the rear. One division of the Red Cross was now domiciled at the convent near Gabrova, where Sallie and Alice had been entertained on their flight from Eski Zagra.

The Damascus roses were blossoming in the greatest profusion in the cloister garden, but the nuns had other work now than the preparation of attar.

James Osborne galloped into the courtyard on the 15th of July, and reported that Gourko had advanced by the Hainkoi. "He will be across the Balkans to-morrow. Captain Müller is in the advance," he said to Sallie. "Gourko has given him an important position. He has sent you this note, for he could not come to say farewell. I am off to join them. And as I am free to ride where I will, you may expect me in a few days, with news of the victory."

He was gone, and Sallie, half-dazed, read the note, —

"LIEBCHEN, — I am off over the pass which you know so well. The fact that you have crossed through it will make it very dear to me. I go with high hopes and good omens. One of our men — a Don Cossack — gave me a scrap of 'bursting weed' this morning, and I have fastened it in my helmet, so, of course, we shall burst through.

"Farewell,
"Thy FRIEDRICH."

Sallie waited in deep anxiety, but one morning James Osborne came with the promised news. The daring raid was a brilliant success. The Turks had not thought of this deep, wild gorge, and had left it absolutely unguarded. So faithful were the Bulgarians that not a man, woman, or child betrayed the coming of the Russians. And though three battalions of Turkish soldiers passed the southern extremity of the defile that night, they did not suspect that eleven thousand Russians were camping, without fires, in that tortuous ravine.

The next morning the army poured into the plain below, and re-enforced by the Bulgarian legion, which Trajan Evanova and men who like him had "Batak!" for their watchword had been gathering at Kezanlik, were enthusiastically greeted and entertained by the Bulgarians of this town. The next day the attack was made upon the rear of Shipka, a complete surprise to the Turks, who had been fighting all the preceding day with Prince Mirsky's division, and who now surrendered, after a sharp combat. Abdul Kerim was a broken man, soon to be degraded from his post as commander. Shipka Pass was won and refortified, — its guns pointing to the south. It was a brilliant achievement, — a marvel of strategy and heroic valor. Encouraged by the success of his dashing raid, General Gourko descended from the mountains, and scoured the country to the south, ignoring the fact that the main Russian army was still on the other side of the Balkans, where they were destined to lie before Plevna for many weary months, while Suleiman Pasha, with his forty thousand reserves, — redifs and spahis, the flower of the Turkish army, — as well as the ferocious Bashi-Bazouks, — were waiting for work to do. Gourko marched on the 29th of July, for forty miles, and fought the Turks at the railroad station of Jeni Zagra, taking it, and destroying an immense mass of stores. The next day he attempted to return to Eski Zagra, not knowing that Suleiman Pasha's men had fallen upon the town and were wreaking on it a terrible revenge for its friendly reception of the Russians. Not till Gourko had come in sight of the city was he warned of what was going on. Even then he wished to pass on to the help of the Bulgarian legion, who had come out so nobly to his aid, and who were beset in the city. But he saw at a glance that this would be simply to throw away his men, and he made a hasty retreat back by the Hainkoi Pass. As for the poor Bulgarian legion, it fought its way back to Shipka, beginning its retreat with sixteen hundred men, and only between four and five hundred reaching the fortifications.

Shipka Pass was gained, but at what a price! The wounded men brought over the terrible Hainkoi Pass, in jolting carts, died by the wagon-load, before they could be transferred to the hospital. Gourko had lost three thousand men, exclusive of the Bulgarians. Captain Müller brought up the rear, as he had before led the advance. The sun poured down its blazing rays, as they traversed the long plain before striking into the shadowy gorge. He thought of the cool ferns; and the drip, drip of the little brook seemed to be sounding in his ears. His eyes felt baked in their sockets, and his brain swam with sleeplessness. Should they never reach the shadows? He lifted his helmet to allow the passage of the air, and the crisp, curling leaves of the dried bursting weed crumbled and fell in powder. The dust was rising on the plain in the rear. Horsemen were galloping toward them. Were they Bulgarians, or Bashi-Bazouks? There was a little puff of smoke along the line, and he reeled in his saddle, clutched at his horse's mane and fell. He was the last man in the column, and the others did not hear or did not heed. Even his horse did not stop and stand over him with the proverbial faithfulness universally ascribed to that intelligent animal. It trotted carelessly on, after its comrades. He could hear their hoof-beats growing fainter, fainter, and then the earth and all therein seemed to fall away from under him,—dying was easier than he had thought! He tried to say, "O God! for Christ's sake pardon my offences." But he was conscious that he only thought the prayer, that he had lost the power of speech; another instant and thought had gone too.

CHAPTER XVI.

PLEVNA, AND THE PASSAGE OF THE BALKANS.

SALLIE was very busy at Gabrova, for the convent was filled now with Gourko's wounded. She had wondered, shudderingly, if she might not see Friedrich Müller's face looking up to her from one of the stretchers which the men brought in, and had thanked God that all were strangers. He had not come back with Gourko, she knew, but she believed him to be at Shipka, until James Osborne came back from the fort one day, and inadvertently inquired for him. He knew by her sudden pallor that Captain Müller was among the lost three thousand.

"He did not come back with his division. He is not among the wounded. He is not at Shipka? Then he must be dead!" She spoke very steadily. But James Osborne was not deceived by her self-possession. "Perhaps he has been taken prisoner," he suggested. She smiled incredulously. "The Turks take no prisoners," she said calmly, and then she turned to the poor Cossack with the gangrened hand, and by long and patient argument persuaded him to its amputation.

The hospital at Gabrova had thinned. Some patients had recovered, a few had died, more were able to be sent to Bucharest. The cots lay white and vacant, and now news came of terrible fighting at Plevna.

Baron Krudener had committed the blunder of letting Osman Pasha and his army occupy this fine strategical point, and now, though nearly the entire Russian force was pitted against the city, they found it impossible to dislodge him. There was incessant work upon parallels and intrenchments creeping nearer and nearer the city. There were terrific bombardments. There were Turkish sallies, and redoubts taken

PASSAGE OF BALKANS.

by the bayonet. But the summer dragged on to its close, and Osman was still unsubdued. The Czar watched the charges with his field-glass, and inspected the lines. The most skilful generals discussed the situation in their councils of war. It would never do to march on to the south and leave Osman behind them. Plevna must be taken before the main army could cross the Balkans. And Gourko and Skobeleff were dashing around Plevna, cutting off Osman's communication with the south, and trusting to the co-operation of the great siege-general — Starvation — to help reduce the city. But the city was evidently well provisioned, and it held out as pluckily as Paris had done in the Franco-Prussian War, hoping for re-enforcements, and for the coming of the Field Marshal Winter, to blockade the Balkan roads and drive the Russians back. A second campaign, the Czar knew, would bankrupt his treasury. The fighting must be finished this winter, and the weary siege continued. There was good news from Asia, where Mukhtar Pasha, who had fought in Herzegovina, was defending Erzeroum, and, it was thought, must soon surrender. But frightful storms were swirling down on the Balkans, and might render them impassable, and the Russians pushed forward the siege with fierce determination. Every day added to the Russian wounded in all the Red Cross hospitals, to which they were forwarded by the surgeons at the front. There was a battle on August 30, resulting in a second defeat; and a third unsuccessful attack in the presence of the Czar, on September 11. Finally, on the night of December 10, Osman Pasha, his supplies exhausted, and his outer defences captured, made a desperate sortie. The battle lasted from daybreak until noon. Much of the time hand to hand — a bayonet contest over the guns of the Russians. But the Turks were driven back, and, in the afternoon, Osman surrendered, and was brought, wounded and a prisoner, before the Czar. Plevna had fallen. The Turkish prisoners of war were sent to Roumania and to Russia, and the Russian army was delirious with joy. All but the dead, who lay unburied in the trenches, and the wounded, who waited for attention, and could not be transferred fast enough to the hospitals. But if the condition of the Russian wounded was distressing, it was not to be compared with the horrible state of things in the Turkish hospitals in Plevna. When the Turks made their sortie, all the hospital attendants followed them, and the sick and wounded were left for three days without care or service. When the Russians finally assumed this duty, over a thousand had died from

FORGOTTEN.

neglect, and were lying beside the living, many of whom were too far gone to be helped by the tardy aid. There was work enough for the Red Cross at Gabrova now. And, though Sallie's heart was almost breaking with her own trouble, she let her tears fall in secret, and labored steadily on. James Osborne worked with the surgeons at the front, in distributing food to the famishing prisoners. One starving crone was so crazed by her sufferings that she cursed him, even while she snatched at the provisions. He labored, too, in the over-crowded hospital-tents, where the wounded received their first temporary treatment, and in front of which they lay, in long rows, waiting for attention, with that pathetic look of uncomplaining patience in their eyes which has been so admirably depicted in the great picture of this scene, by the Russian artist Verestchagin. One day he appeared, with a detachment of wounded, at the hospital where Sallie was working. He was shocked by her changed appearance, — her sunken eyes and thin, trembling hands. "You will kill yourself!" he cried. "You are over-working cruelly."

"I suppose I do not sleep enough," she replied. "But how can one sleep when there is so much to be done? I am working in the fever-ward."

"Yes, and you will take it yourself, and we shall lose a valuable nurse. You require an immediate change. I am going to cross the Balkans with Skobeleff. We can take a very few nurses, with two ambulances. Will you come with us? There will be work enough to do when we reach the other side, — perhaps before."

TURKISH CRONE.

"Yes, let me go," Sallie replied. "Friedrich is across the Balkans."

James Osborne looked up quickly. Had she any hope? She spoke too steadily for that.

"My poor child!" he said, "you have suffered cruelly, but have faith. All of this death means the resurrection of the land, and you have given and done for that end all that woman can."

"If I could have your faith," Sallie said, "that such evil means could ever work out a good end."

"'Bate not one jot of faith and hope,'" said James Osborne cheerily. "'It is always the darkest just before day.' And Alice is over the Balkans somewhere. You know Lady Strangford went out from

England and organized a society like ours, for the care of the Turkish wounded, called the Red Crescent. Lady Saunters and Alice are working in it; and if we may judge of other Turkish hospitals by those of Plevna, they have more to do than we."

Heavy storms delayed for a time the advance; but on Christmas Day, General Gourko, with an army of thirty thousand men, set out for a second crossing of the Balkans, *via* Sofia and Trajan's Pass, while General Skobeleff led his men to a second storming of Shipka Pass, which had been retaken by Suleiman Pasha. Both movements were successful, though performed in the face of terrific storms. The men wore great-coats with pointed hoods pulled over their heads, and icicles hung from their mustaches, giving them the appearance of so many Santa Clauses.

A band of medical students were given their choice of going behind or marching on foot, and unanimously chose to take their chances with the infantry, and were on hand and did noble service at the next battle.

Sallie made the crossing with two Sisters of Charity, perched on the top of a wagon loaded with knitted socks, waistbands, and jerseys, which she helped distribute to the frost-bitten men. Sentries were frozen to death, and hundreds of men on the hospital list with frost-bitten hands and feet.

There was hard fighting at Shipka Pass again, and many wounded; and it was long before Sallie reached Kezanlik, now occupied by Prince Mirsky, but only the wreck of the beautiful town through which she had passed on leaving the country.

How could James Osborne maintain such an unwavering and cheerful faith through it all! Her hand stole to her pocket Testament. She would read a little from that wonderful chapter on faith. "Women received their dead raised to life again," were the first words that greeted her. And she smiled bitterly, for the verse seemed to mock at her. "Oh, yes! it were easy to have faith on such terms.

But of how many of the poor women about her could this be said?" She read on, "And others were tortured." Here at last was something for her. "Not accepting deliverance, that they might obtain a better resurrection." That was what James Osborne had meant — the resurrection of the nation. Over one of the shattered houses the Red

RELIEVING THE GUARD AT SHIPKA.

Crescent was flying. Some one stood in the doorless aperture, — some one who was not a Turk, though he wore a scarlet fez, and a crescent of the same color on his arm. Nor was he a Russian, though the rest of his dress was that of a European. From a distance the figure seemed familiar, and as he turned she recognized the face of Algernon Saunters. He came forward and greeted her with grave politeness. "My mother is within," he said, "and your friend Alice

Newton. Come in and rest. You are ill. You are only the shadow of your former self!"

"That is just what I was thinking of you," Sallie replied with a faint smile.

Lady Saunters and Alice greeted Sallie warmly. And they sat down together in a room which had been a stable, and was now used as the hospital kitchen, and talked over the experiences of the campaign, and the outlook for the future.

"The war is virtually ended," said Algernon. "Now that the Russians have passed the Balkans, Suleiman Pasha and his army are fleeing for Constantinople, with Gourko in hot pursuit. Peace negotiations will soon begin."

"And what has this poor country gained?" Sallie asked mournfully.

"The country is impoverished," Alice replied. "O Sallie! you should see the deserted homes which I have visited, and hear the poor women, who have crept back to them, wailing by their hearthstones, 'Oh, my sweet home! my sweet home! Oh, my husband! my dear husband! Oh, my children! my pretty children!' There are some who have lost all. The English and Americans have collected the orphans from Batak and other desolated villages, and are caring for them. Mr. Schuyler obtained a list of eighty-seven children, who had been sold, and has had them given up. I saw many of them at Philippopolis. And little Ghiorghy and Anghel, the younger brothers of poor Marika and Katarinka, were among them."

"Perhaps," said Sallie, "as James Osborne hopes, a new national life will be born from all this struggle. But it seems hardly possible that its advantages will be such as to repay for all this horror of bloodshed and suffering."

"The future will tell," said Algernon sadly. "I confess that I am not over-sanguine. But of one thing I am certain: if the civilized world at large could only realize what this war has meant, what any war means, this would be the last sanctioned by Christian countries, and arbitration would be instantly agreed upon."

They were silent for a few moments. Lady Saunters and Alice had hurried away to their patients, and at length Algernon asked, "Do you know what brought me here? I resigned my position in the India service, on account of a disordered liver. To have told the truth, the resignation should have read, a disordered conscience. Your talk at Athens rankled within me like slow poison. And when this war was declared, I came home to see if I could not get a diplomatic position. I think I shall have one when affairs are settled, and I'll do my best to heal these wounds. But, meantime, I could find nothing better to do than to come out here with mother. They call the English Turkish sympathizers, and, I confess, we do sympathize with their sufferings. You must see our hospital. We have one patient who ought to be transferred to the Red Cross, — a young Russian, — who has lain for months between life and death."

"A Russian in a Turkish hospital! How was that possible?"

"Only through guile on my part. The story may interest you. You remember Norcross?"

"The thief and renegade? Yes!"

"Hush! the poor fellow is dead. He was wounded at the beginning of the war, on the Danube. He was brought on his ironclad to Burgas; and, hearing there that there were English physicians here, he refused to submit himself to Turkish surgeons, and insisted on being transported to our hospital. We did our best to save him. But his wound had been too long neglected. And he died on the night that the Bashi-Bazouks retook this place, and slaughtered the Bulgarian legion in the streets. It was a horrible night. And he heard the cries and shouts as he lay dying. Our attendants deserted us. But the hospital was not disturbed. Two days later a Bulgarian swineherd told me that he had found a wounded Russian officer, — one of Gourko's men, lost on his retreat to the Balkans, and had hidden him in his hut. I went out with the man after nightfall with a stretcher, and brought him in, having first dressed him as a Turk. He was blond, and unmistakably European in appearance. But we laid him on Norcross's pallet, and when the attendants came back they, and all Turks who visited the hospital, believed that he was the White Pasha. He is recovering rapidly now. Come and see him, for he belongs to you."

Sallie turned quickly. "What did you say?"

"I mean that he is a Russian, and, as such, should be transferred to your hospital."

Sallie did not hear, but followed quickly. On a pallet was stretched the gaunt form of the man she had mourned as dead. He was sleeping, and she sunk noiselessly upon her knees by his side. Algernon looked at her in astonishment. "You were right. He belongs to me," she said simply. "In spite of my little faith, I have received my dead raised to life again."

Algernon Saunters knew instantly that his hope was vain.

Meanwhile, James Osborne had taken the camp-fever, and lay dying. He heard the booming of the cannon, as they celebrated the declaration of peace, and asked, "Are they fighting again?"

"No," said Melicent, "the End has come, and Bulgaria is free!"

A sunny smile swept over his face. "Then, how can you ask, my wife, whether it has all paid?"

But Melicent, a widow when scarcely a bride; and Sallie, who tasted the same cup of sorrow, though it was mercifully removed; and Alice, who saw her lessons of love, forgiveness of injuries, and meekness, rudely set aside, and revenge paraded as the Christian mode of solving difficulties; and thousands of bereaved women and children ask, — Is there no better way?

www.ingramcontent.com/pod-product-compliance
Lightning Source LLC
Chambersburg PA
CBHW021807230426
43669CB00008B/654